The Proper Care of
GOLDFISH

TW 107S

This book is dedicated to Burkhard Kahl, who makes such beautiful photographs of all kinds of fishes, especially goldfish.

© **T.F.H. Publications, Inc.**

Distributed in the UNITED STATES to the Pet Trade by T.F.H. Publications, Inc., 1 TFH Plaza, Neptune City, NJ 07753; on the Internet at www.tfh.com; in CANADA by Rolf C. Hagen Inc., 3225 Sartelon St., Montreal, Quebec H4R 1E8; Pet Trade by H & L Pet Supplies Inc., 27 Kingston Crescent, Kitchener, Ontario N2B 2T6; in ENGLAND by T.F.H. Publications, PO Box 74, Havant PO9 5TT; in AUSTRALIA AND THE SOUTH PACIFIC by T.F.H. (Australia), Pty. Ltd., Box 149, Brookvale 2100 N.S.W., Australia; in NEW ZEALAND by Brooklands Aquarium Ltd., 5 McGiven Drive, New Plymouth, RD1 New Zealand; in SOUTH AFRICA by Rolf C. Hagen S.A. (PTY.) LTD., P.O. Box 201199, Durban North 4016, South Africa; in JAPAN by T.F.H. Publications. Published by T.F.H. Publications, Inc.

MANUFACTURED IN THE
UNITED STATES OF AMERICA
BY T.F.H. PUBLICATIONS, INC.

The Proper Care of
GOLDFISH

JAMES GERAN

Overleaf: *A female ryukin with good body form. This is an easy variety for the beginner.* **Below:** *A Black Lionhead,* Carassius auratus. *Photo by Michael Gilroy.*

Contents

This is a very rare black and orange telescope veitail. It might also be called a broadtail, because the names given to goldfish may be subject to variation. Each country and each group of goldfish enthusiasts may define the characteristics of a give variety differently. Photo: Fred Rosenzweig

Introduction

There are thought to be about 25,000 fish species found in the various waters of our planet, and if a survey were to be done to find the most well known of these, it would probably be the common goldfish. Many fish are, of course, known to the populations of different countries because fish form a staple part of many diets, but the species eaten vary considerably from one part of the world to the other; the goldfish is totally cosmopolitan and as a pet ranks alongside the dog, the cat, and the budgerigar as one of the world's most popular household choices. In terms of gross numbers kept, the goldfish is possibly the world's number one pet, because those who keep them tend to have more than one. In some cases hundreds may be found in the home of a dedicated enthusiast.

The choice of a fish as a pet is perhaps surprising at first, because you cannot stroke it or talk to it. You cannot take a fish for a walk or play with it or teach it to do tricks, so why are we attracted to these creatures from the depths of what is to us an alien world—water? The reasons are many. For one thing, all land animals originally came from the water many millions of years ago, and a feature of mammals is that at some stage in their embryonic development they still retain aquatic features—humans possess gill arches, for example, when they are developing in the mother's womb. Water is vital to life itself, so it is natural that we should be interested in anything that lives in it. The very fact that fish are neither demanding—nor noisy—is a considerable advantage to them as pets. It means they can be kept in places where other pets might not be appreciated or would be more of a problem to maintain well—in high-rise apartments, for example.

It is a proven fact that parents. An aquarium that is well furnished has a tranquility about it that is very restful after a tiring day, and there is no doubt that it has a therapeutic value in reducing stress.

New goldfish strains are appearing every year. These black moors won a prize in Singapore. They are totally black except for rusty undersides and have a long dorsal and a split but long tail. Photo: Dr. Herbert R. Axelrod

having to care for another life form is important in a stable psychological makeup, and certainly where children are concerned it helps them to develop a real sense of responsibility under the guiding influence of their Of course, the main reason why people keep fish is because of their intrinsic beauty as well as because of the beautiful furnished containers in which they are housed. Over the centuries many species of fish have been kept, and while

This is a rather poor specimen of a water bubble-eye. The lumps on the back are vestigial dorsal fin rays. The color is interesting because it is rare, but it is not very attractive.

the goldfish is the most common—this term also being used to describe the most popular variety of this species—it is also the most regal of all fish kept by humans. The first cultivated domestic pet fish were almost certainly goldfish, and they were highly regarded by the nobility of China and of other Far Eastern countries such as Japan. As the centuries rolled by, more ornate varieties were developed. These were exported to Europe and thence to the USA and Australia, to be kept initially by the more wealthy families but in more recent times by any person wanting to maintain a hardy yet very attractive fish in the home.

With a growing awareness of the needs of fish, it became possible to keep both tropical and marine specimens, and these species have developed into an enormous separate hobby. However, in spite of the fierce competition from tropical fish, the goldfish has maintained its position as the most popular species to keep. Indeed, the keeping of coldwater species generally is enjoying somewhat of a boom at this time, helped no doubt by the increasing number of people who now own outdoor ponds.

A golden Chinese lionhead goldfish. Photo: Fred Rosenzweig

In spite of the great strides made in aquarium technology, it is a sad fact that old ideas take a long while to die out. As a result there are still far too many goldfish being kept under what amounts to primitive conditions in which they have little hope of leading contented, stress-free lives. The reasons for this situation are two-fold. On the one hand, goldfish are extremely hardy animals capable of withstanding conditions that would certainly kill most other fish of comparable beauty, while on the other hand, the concept that goldfish are cheap to keep and maintain, and to purchase, has led to the notion that these fish can be kept in just about any sort of container—and in particular that most unsuitable of all containers, the goldfish bowl.

When the poor goldfish dies, people simply shrug their shoulders and go out and buy another fish or two rather than stop to consider why the fish keep dying. The very low price of goldfish has thus been their worst enemy, because it devalues their very life, a sad but true fact which can be equally applied to most pets in their basic forms. Matters are not helped by the number of unsuitable containers produced and marketed for the keeping of fish.

Let me depart from the usual advice to "buy a goldfish because they are so inexpensive to start up with." A well furnished coldwater aquarium need not be costly, but if it is to be worthwhile then, overall, it might cost as much as a pedigreed puppy or kitten and somewhat more than the cost of a couple of good budgerigars and a quality cage for them. If you think only in terms of a goldfish bowl or a similar small unit which contains a quantity of gravel and a plastic galleon, then you will not derive any great pleasure from your purchase, and the goldfish will not look their best for long, nor will they be contented and so will probably die well short of their potential life span.

On the other hand, a well planned small aquarium of

Top view of lionhead goldfish.

reasonable quality will not only look better but will last for a great number of years. If it is furnished with needed equipment the water will remain clear and fresh, and in turn the goldfish will retain their color and their health so that both the fish and you can enjoy the benefits that you can give to each other.

Goldfish have been bred from ancient times to be viewed from above. Thus their beauty is judged from a top view. Photo: Burkhard Kahl

Selecting an Aquarium

The choice of aquarium is obviously fundamental to the keeping of any fish species. It will contain the entire boundaries of the fish's world, and just how pleasant that world is for your goldfish will be determined by your decision over the size and shape of the aquarium. From that already discussed, it is to be hoped that small goldfish bowls will not be a consideration at all, because their only real value

THE ANATOMY OF THE GOLDFISH.

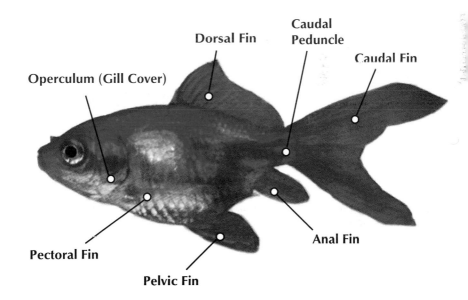

Operculum (Gill Cover)
Dorsal Fin
Caudal Peduncle
Caudal Fin
Pectoral Fin
Pelvic Fin
Anal Fin

當盛江戸鹿子

Japanese art often includes goldfish among its themes. Goldfish have long been a prominent part of Japanese life.

would likely present more problems than was justified by its size. It must be appreciated that the smaller the volume of contained water, the more rapidly this can degenerate. Large tanks are always much easier to maintain in healthy states, so purchase the largest unit you can afford.

SHAPE

There has been a rapid development in the shape of aquariums available from which you can choose. Your local dealer might have round, triangular, and even hexagonal tanks, but, as interesting as these may look, the well-known rectangular shape remains the most popular and practical. It

is as a temporary holding receptacle or as a place in which to keep a few plants.

The very minimum size for an aquarium would be about 60 x 30 x 38cm wide (24 x 12 x 15 inches); anything smaller should be regarded as unsuitable for coldwater species and

affords an excellent frontal viewing area and it has a first class surface area in relation to water volume contained—and this is the most important consideration as far as stocking levels go. Round aquariums give a distorted view of the fish, while triangular shapes will not house the number of inmates that the frontal area might suggest. Tall aquariums have a poor surface/volume ratio, and maintaining good aeration in them can only be achieved with ancillary equipment. They are very impractical units, especially for coldwater species.

The Japanese and Chinese kept goldfish in tubs and vats where they could be viewed with ease from above. This explains the emphasis even today on appearance from the top rather than the sides.

MATERIALS

Numerous synthetic compounds, such as Plexiglas, are used to produce long-lasting aquariums—the better acrylics now available are far better than in past years, but the non-scratch quality

Today keeping goldfish remains a popular and relatively inexpensive hobby attractive to all ages. New techniques and equipment have improved the appearance of the goldfish aquarium, and the goldfish themselves are available in a broader range of colors and varieties. Photo: Dr. Herbert R. Axelrod

tanks of this material will be costly. The others tend to scratch easily when cleaned and rapidly become yellow with use. They also tend to bow more readily, especially larger units made inexpensively.

Glass remains a good material to have for your tank, as it has good clarity, cleans easily, and will last for many years. Indeed, the glass aquarium that is well sealed when manufactured will arguably last a lifetime. It is, of course, possible for handy people to make their own tank to fit into a particular space, but this can work out more expensively than shopping around for a suitably sized unit. Another factor that should be remembered about home-made units is that you might just find it impossible to

Antique goldfish aquariums typically were ornate and often formed centerpieces in the ornately furnished rooms of the period.

Whatever else you do, start with an all-glass or acrylic tank of recent manufacture. These sturdy and attractive tanks are a great improvement over both the unhealthy goldfish bowls and heavy metal-framed aquariums of the past. Photo:. Dr. Herbert R. Axelrod

purchase a suitable canopy, whereas those sold in aquatic shops will have ready-made canopies for them.

The greater the volume of water, the more pressure it exerts on the glass or acrylic walls, so clearly as tank size increases so must the thickness of the walls. The larger tanks will normally have cross members from front to back on them for extra strength. The base is always somewhat thicker than the side walls.

A final comment in respect to aquarium materials is that in any tanks that are bonded (as opposed to molded one-piece units), make sure they do not leak. Just occasionally a tank may have a fault, though all good units are tested before being offered for sale. The other point to check on is that the glass is without flaw—again it is in the cheaper models that defects are more likely to be apparent. By flaw is meant any distortion to the glass or any chipped edges; these should be beveled so there is no risk that you might cut yourself on them.

WATER VOLUME

It is important that you know the volume of water an aquarium will hold, because this will be needed should medications be added. Also, the size of water pump needed will be governed by volume and, finally, you will want to

TANK SIZES AND GLASS THICKNESS

TANK	GLASS	VOLUME (liters)	(U.S. Gallons)
60 x 30 x 38cm (24 x 12 x 15 in)	6mm (1/4 in)	64	17
90 x 38 x 30cm (36 x 15 x 12 in)	6mm (1/4 in)	103	28
150 x 45 x 45cm (60 x 18 x 18 in)	12mm (1/2 in)	304	80

Large aquariums can be made to order from acrylics. Photo courtesy of AAMPRo, Las Vegas, Nevada

know just how heavy the aquarium will be so that when it is sited you do not risk its crashing through a cupboard or other unit it is placed on. Water is heavy.

To calculate the volume, multiply the length x depth x width. As an example, an aquarium 60x30x38cm has a cubic centimeter capacity of 68,400. There are 1000 cubic centimeters in a liter, so the tank will hold 68.4 liters of water. Conversion of liters to imperial or U.S. gallons is a simple multiplication:

Stands for aquariums come in many sizes and designs to fit any tanks and any room decor.

A liter equals 0.264 US gallons, thus 68.4 liters = 18 US gallons;

A liter equals 0.22 Imperial gallons, thus 68.4 liters = 15 imperial gallons.

In view of the difference between the Imperial (UK) gallon and that of the US, and given the extensive trade between the two nations, readers should be aware of a few conversions, because it has been noted that manufacturers do not always point out such differences and obviously these are very important.

One UK gallon = 1.2 US gallons

One US gallon = 0.833 UK gallons or 5/6 of a UK gallon

In order to complete the series, the following are useful metric conversions:

One UK gallon = 4.55 liters

One US gallon = 3.785 liters.

WATER WEIGHT

Having established the volume of the water, the next thing is to convert this to weight, for which the following will be useful:

A gallon of water weighs 10 pounds (UK) =4.55 kilograms; 8.345 pounds (US)=3.79 kilograms.

A liter of water weighs 1 kg or 2.2 lbs.

Thus the specimen tank cited has a water weight of

With adult supervision, even children can set up a tank satisfactory for keeping goldfish. Many products to make the tank more attractive are available at your pet shop.

68.4 kilos or 150 lb., which is equivalent to the weight of an average adult person, so it is quite a weight when you consider it is by no means a very large aquarium. Do not forget that to this must be added the weight of the tank itself plus the weight of the gravel, rocks, and fitments, less the water they displace and any capacity not taken up (you would never fill an aquarium to the brim). In general, you can figure the weight of a filled tank at 10 pounds per gallon of tank capacity (US), 12 pounds per gallon (UK).

TANK DEPTH

It is the surface area of the aquarium that will control the number of fish that can be kept; the depth has little bearing on the oxygen content. However, depth is not unimportant to an aquarium, especially

Although many fancy and expensive goldfish are available, many people are satisfied with "typical" goldfish of mixed heritage. Long tail fins seem to be preferred regardless of color or head type. Photo: Burkhard Kahl

Rectangular tanks are the shape most commonly seen used for aquariums, but tanks in the form of other regular polygons, such as hexagons and octagons, also are available.

when species other than goldfish are included. It provides swimming space for the fish and also affords them space to avoid more aggressive individuals, which one always finds in any community of animals. Varieties such as the veiltails are in danger of having their fins nipped if they do not have sufficient space to occupy their own territory. They are not as fast as some varieties and can find themselves harassed in small aquariums containing mixed groups of goldfish. Of course, especially aggressive individuals should be removed. A good depth of water will allow you to make an interesting aquascene, but do ensure the length of the tank is proportionate to the depth.

There are a few goldfish varieties which are as interesting when viewed from above as when they are seen from the side, so it can occasionally be desirable to have shallow aquariums. With this in mind, we may well see a shift in conventional thinking in the coming years as a result of this factor and the increasing interest in color breeding and hybridization with koi in order to transfer long fins to the koi and colors to the goldfish.

SITING THE TANK

Having made all the calculations and decided upon the aquarium to be purchased, the next decision will be where to place it. It must be placed where it will not be subjected to drafts or to strong sunlight. Apart from overheating the aquarium, sunlight will encourage the growth of algae on the front viewing panel of glass. Obviously the weight of the furnished unit is a major consideration, so it must be placed on a very solid surface indeed. With a very tall and very narrow stand you would be wise to en-

sure that the stand itself is either screwed to the wall or in some other way secured to it so there is no danger that it could topple over by accident.

The aquarium is safe as long as the base is on a perfectly flat surface, and in order to iron out any small irregularities, it is better if you place it on a layer of cork or on polystyrene tiles, both of which will cushion the weight so that the pressure of the water on the base is evenly spread.

For practical purposes the tank should be placed in proximity to a power point so that electrical fitments can easily be plugged in. There are a number of companies who specialize in supplying cabinets for aquariums, and such units are made from attractive woods and styled to period or modern fashions as required. Another aspect that should be considered when siting an aquarium is the fact that you want to look at it. This being so, its height

Most goldfish keepers prefer fish with bright, even brilliant, colors. Specialists often keep fish with subdued colors if other features are of interest to them. Photo: Andre Roth

from the floor should be such that you have a good view from your most favored seat but it should not be so high that servicing becomes difficult. In many instances the location ends up as a compromise which must take account of the design of the room. It should be added that a kitchen is not a good place to accommodate an aquarium, though I have seen many so placed. The problem is that this is one room where there tend to be a lot of dust and potentially toxic fumes. It happens that the very aquariums I have seen in kitchens are always the small ones which have no filters, aeration, etc., and which are thus the least able to cope with such an atmosphere.

Should it be impossible for you to avoid a site that gets quite a lot of sunlight which would fall directly onto the aquarium, you can overcome the problem to a degree by blotting out the sun on that side of the tank with one of many materials, including those specially made for aquariums.

If you have purchased a good-sized aquarium and really want it to be an attractive feature in your home, then it is essential that it is provided with good lighting—you really would be amazed at the transformation this makes to even a small unit, apart from which light is vital to plant growth.

A rare black bubble-eye with good coloration and large eye sacs. Photo: Fred Rosenzweig

The Garden Pond

The number of people who today have a garden pond is larger than ever before. Indeed, the interest in the outdoor cold-water side of aquatics is the most rapidly expanding section of the overall hobby. There is little doubt that Japanese koi are responsible for much of this increased interest, but not all of it, and goldfish have a very healthy following among pond owners and have been the mainstay of this aspect of freshwater fish keeping for many years. One advantage goldfish have over koi is that they do not grow as large and as a result you will not be faced with the decision of having to part with them because they have outgrown their pond. They will also be less expensive to purchase.

Not all goldfish varieties are suited to life in a pond. Those which are can be divided between those which can safely be left year 'round in the pond and those which are better wintered indoors—depending on whether or not you live in a warm climate.

In terms of its management, a garden pond is much like an aquarium, for it is after all only a container of water but on a much larger scale. Being outdoors is both advantageous and a negative at one and the same time. Being much larger, it will accommodate more and larger goldfish, and the water condition will not change as rapidly as will that of the aquarium. The temperature will also stay more constant and the whole environment is much more like a natural habitat than is the aquarium. On the negative side, it is obviously considerably more expensive to in-

A large Japanese garden pool. This photo was taken in Kyoto, Japan, and shows the simple beauty of Japanese ponds. Photo: Guido Dingerkus

stall and your view of the goldfish is from the top rather than from the side. While an aquarium can be serviced at night be-cause it is indoors, it is less convenient to do this at such a time with a pond, which will require daytime attention.

An informal British garden pool. Space limitations on most backyard pools often yield a cluttered appearance that can be distracting to the viewer. Photo: Michael Gilroy

Overall, the pond is more demanding of your time, but then a well prepared pond and its surrounds are undoubtedly an added feature to any garden and it provides a restful way to spend a day or a few hours after work. It is the gentle beauty of water and fish that has no doubt been responsible for the increase in the number of pond owners. With added lighting you can spend many an evening around a pond and enjoy the tranquil setting. The virtues of ponds have of course been appreciated by the Chinese and Japanese for many centuries while even in Western countries the art of keeping goldfish in ponds is a very old hobby associated with the more wealthy families and their stately homes.

The availability of plastic and synthetic rubber compounds has revolutionized pond construction and brought it within the reach of just about any family today. You do not need a vast yard or garden to have a pond, and with the correct filtration system much of the hard work

An elaborate garden pond complete with a bridge. To some people the straight sides of the pond detract from its beauty. Photo: Hugh Nicholas

associated with ponds of yesteryear has vanished.

INITIAL PLANNING

The first stage in having a garden pond is to plan out every aspect in some detail. Unlike an aquarium you cannot just move a pond at your leisure, so it is important that matters are all considered at length and in this way you are less likely to end up with some-thing that you later regret. There are many things to consider and the first of these is where the pond is to be sited. Next will be the material that the pond is to be made of and then how the pond will be filtered. These are the major decisions, but obviously along with these will be the question of how large a pond you require. Is it to be raised or sunken, of formal or informal shape, will it contain plants and how near to your home would you like it to be? We will briefly look at each of these aspects so that a would-be owner is aware of many of the potential pitfalls that can and do befall owners who rush into pond installation.

THE POND SITE

If we work on the assumption that your interest in ponds is to contain goldfish, rather than simply be a part of an overall garden setting, then the best place to site a pond is as near to your home as you can manage. In this way you will be able to see your fish from the comfort of your living room on those less than sunny days; at the same time, routine jobs will not become a chore and are more easily accomplished if everything is close at hand.

A koi and goldfish pond in a Japanese garden. This Is a very simple but effective layout.

The site should enjoy some protection from cold winds in order to maintain reasonably constant temperatures, this being more important in raised pools than in those which are sunk into the earth. The site should not be overhung by tree branches which will pollute the water with the sap they extrude, with the feces of birds perched in them, and with the falling leaves of autumn. Beyond these aspects, the roots of trees always move in the direction of water and they could thus cause some damage to the pond surrounds—and the pond itself, were it to be made of concrete.

By being close to the home installation, costs will be lower because you will not need such long lengths of piping to connect to the filter system and to the electrical supply and drains. However, one consideration likely to apply to a site near to

A small amount of vegetation on the edge of the goldfish pond produces a more natural look as well as attracting insects that will supplement the diet of the fish. Photo: Dr. Herbert R. Axelrod

In the tropics, goldfish ponds may face the problems of dangerous algal blooms and high water temperatures through much of the year. Photo: Dr. Herbert R. Axelrod

the home that is less likely to apply if the pond is at a distance is that of its being over utility services, which obviously cannot be allowed to happen. Check out your sewage, electric, and water piping positions so you know where you cannot place the pond. If you do decide to site the pond in the garden at a distance from your home, then choose a low position so the pond looks natural.

SIZE

While you will not be thinking in terms of a pond you could sail a boat on, you should not make the mistake of having it too small, which many owners do and later regret. Remember the comments about small aquariums being more difficult to maintain than large ones; the same applies to a pond. Obviously, you will have some thoughts on the size, so I will say only to make

Many fine products are available for conditioning and treating the water in a pond—very important considerations in the health of the pond's inhabitants. Photo courtesy of Aquarium Pharmaceuticals, Inc.

the actual pond a little larger than perhaps what you are thinking of and then you will probably be delighted with the end result. As with aquariums, the surface area will determine the number of goldfish you can keep in the pool; a good rule of thumb is 30cm (12in) of fish, not counting the tail, to every 0.19m² (2ft²) . This is a safe stocking level that can be increased with moderate aeration and filtration, but this carries risks should the aeration system fail. Most novice pond owners fall into the trap of overstocking their ponds with the result that their fish never reach either the size or the quality of those kept in smaller numbers. The key to success with any cold-water species is to concentrate on fewer fish which are kept under ideal conditions.

The depth of the pond should be at least 1.2 meters (4 ft) across part of its base if you plan to let the goldfish overwinter in the pond. Any shallower than this and in a hard winter you will be counting the dead bodies! Many small pre-fabricated ponds are just too shallow to accommodate goldfish during winters unless the pond is heated. They are also not without problems during hot summers, so bear this in mind if looking at such units. The depth is essential in order that the water does not freeze to the bottom or become too hot in the warmer months.

SHAPE

The choice of shape essentially lies between formal and informal. The former is well suited to gardens which are of a geometric layout with well defined borders to lawns and flower beds. Formal shapes are also more frequently used in raised

The sight of several large goldfish swimming gracefully through a pond has always been relaxing and may be the major reason aquarists build garden ponds. Photo: Dr. Herbert R. Axelrod

ponds because construction is so much more straightforward. The informal pond is suited to the more rambling garden where things do not appear to have been planned. Likewise, if you like Chinese style gardens, an informal pond is more appropriate but can be more difficult to have as a pond close to the home where semi-raised ponds are the more normal.

SUNKEN OR RAISED?

The sunken pond is obviously more natural, and it is easier to have an informal shape to it. It retains its heat better and is much easier to landscape. However, its construction is more difficult because you must dig deeper into the ground for both the pond itself and of course for the filtration piping and bottom drains (if the latter are to be fitted).

The raised pond, or rather partly raised pond, must have very strong supporting walls and should have some protection from cold winds. It is invariably easier to feature a raised pond near the home, and diggings need not be so extensive. Overall, the vast majority of specialty goldfish (and koi) ponds these days are of formal raised types if they are close to homes. Being close to a home does enable one to provide overhead protec-

tion to the pond from direct sunlight simply by running poles from the house wall, and most ponds are better for having some measure of shade to them for, strange as it may seem, goldfish can

This heavily planted garden pond may be very attractive, but the dense vegetation on the surface will make it hard to see the goldfish that inhabit it. Photo: P. Hodgkinson

suffer from sunburn, apart from which excess heat will cause them to lose color during the summer—which is exactly when you will spend most time by the pond.

MATERIALS

In past years cement and concrete were the standard materials for garden ponds. Today these are no longer favored choices because of the time they need to be used for constructing a pond and because they are subject to leaks as well as leaching out lime into the water unless they are constructed to a very high standard. Of course, a really well made concrete pond will last a lifetime and is easily fashioned into any shape; nonetheless they are much less frequently seen these days, primarily because of the growing popularity of the materials that have superseded them.

BUTYL RUBBER LINERS

A good choice for a pond liner is a quality butyl liner,

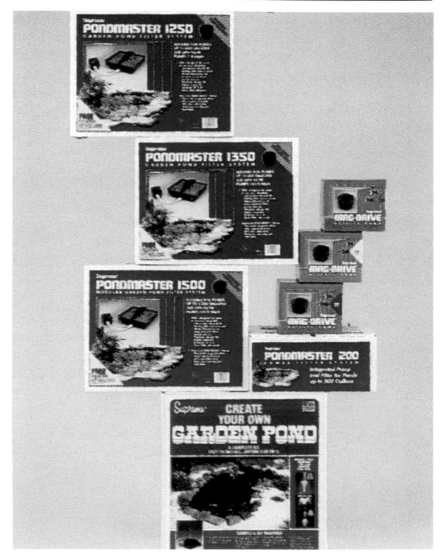

Like indoor aquariums, garden ponds for goldfish can be filtered and aerated with equipment available at pet shops.

for it has long life combined with durability in terms of being able to withstand wear without ripping. Many ponds constructed these days are made of this material. It is sold by the square meter or square foot. Butyl is more expensive than other forms of pond liner, but some owners favor it.

PVC AND POLYETHYLENE LINERS

Polyvinyl chloride (PVC) and polyethylene liners are less expensive than butyl but are less durable, so more care is needed with their installation (but this does not mean butyl should not be handled with care as well). They come in various grades and are available in many different sizes. Their life expectancy is not as long as butyl, but the better grades may last for many years.

PREFORMED PONDS

Molded ponds can be made of rigid PVC, polyester or fiberglass—the latter being very hardy if of good

If you live in an area where your pond is likely to freeze in the winter, you will want to slope the sides. Sloped sides (top drawing) allow the ice to expand without damaging the sides, as is likely to happen with straight sides (bottom drawing) where expanding ice can cause tremendous pressure on the concrete bricks.

quality. The majority of preformed ponds are small, but it is possible to purchase very large ones to order or have them made to one's own requirements, but this would work out to be very expensive. Many are too shallow and the shelves on them are too small. Choose the larger sizes at your dealer's because you will find that, once in the ground, they really do look much smaller than when you view them as complete units.

RENDERED BRICKWORK

An alternative to liners would be to construct a pond from bricks and then to render this construction waterproof with either concrete or fiberglass. In such cases the concrete need not be so thick as would be required in an all-concrete pond, and this method is obviously very suitable for partly raised ponds. Indeed, most liner ponds of raised types have a basic brickwork construction. The use of fiberglass for rendering is not yet very popular and

really needs to be done by professionals, but it is long lasting and very tough.

OTHER ALTERNATIVES

Beyond conventional methods and materials for pond construction, it is always possible that you may have a swimming pool which is rarely used. This would convert to a fine pond. Children's paddling pools may also be utilized as ponds if they are large enough and if they are sunk into the ground to afford protection to their sides.

CALCULATING LINER SIZE

In order that you can estimate the cost of the pond you have in mind, the liner size required is calculated as follows:

Length + twice the depth by width + twice the depth.

You should add 30cm (12in) onto each of the depth figures so that allowance has been made for a generous overlap of liner which will be hidden under slabs or similar edging to the pond. You will find that when compared to the actual surface area, the size of the liner seems enormous, but this is because the depth really does swallow up a lot of liner. Do not be tempted to reduce the depth on this account. Clearly, informal ponds are more difficult to work out, so for an approximation take the nearest square or rectangular sizes the shape will fit into.

VOLUME

The volume of the pond will need to be known both for determining the size of pump and for occasions when medicines are added to the water. There are 1,000 cubic centimeters in a liter, so the formula is length x width x depth (in meters) x 1,000 = number of liters. A pond which is 5 x 3 x 1.5 m will thus contain 22.5 x 1,000 liters of water. This is thus 5,940 US gallons or 4,948 UK gallons, approximately. Useful capacities to know in relation to ponds are as follows:

1 cubic meter = 264.2 US gallons or 220 UK gallons;

1 cubic foot = 7.481 US gallons or 6.23 UK gallons;

1 cubic meter = 35.3147 cubic feet.

In a simple garden pond the liner should be cut wide enough to have excess on the sides to allow for the weight of the water pulling down the liner. The excess can be covered by decorative stone pieces.

Aeration and Circulation

All of the higher life forms require oxygen in order to live, and in the case of fish it is obtained by extraction from the water they inhabit. The amount of oxygen in a given volume of water is determined by many factors, and it is the object of a good aquarist to arrange the aquarium in such a way as to ensure that the water is never deficient in this precious gas. We have no problems with our oxygen supply, because oxygen is about one fifth of our atmosphere, but in water things are very different; the oxygen content may be thousands of times less rich, and this is in well aerated water. Stagnant ponds may have virtually no oxygen at all,

An attractive but common and simple variety is the Japanese ribbontail, a type of ryukin.

and consequently aerobic organisms could not survive in them. An aquarium may be regarded as a stagnant pond for all practical purposes, and the only thing which makes it a potentially viable habitat is our own efforts to overcome its inherent problems.

Oxygen is needed by very many animals and plants, so these will all be competing with your fish for this element. Plants, however, are beneficial because during the process of photosynthesis they release more oxygen than they consume. The other animals mentioned are, of course, the thousands of species of microorganisms that are always present in, and are vital to, any volume of water. During the process of oxidization of waste products and the breakdown of organic matter, oxygen is again consumed, so conditions in a container of water can quickly degenerate if it is left unattended.

A nice group of Chinese calico lionheads. Note the absence of the dorsal fin, typical of lionheads. Photo: Fred Rosenzweig

Apart from these factors, temperature also affects the amount of oxygen a given water volume can contain and a very approximate guide will underline this. At zero degrees centigrade fresh water may hold 10.3ml of oxygen per liter; at 15°C (59°F) this falls to 7.2ml and by about 25°C (77° F) it has decreased to around 6.2ml. In an unaerated aquarium, or pond, this temperature fluctuation can make the difference between life and death and is far more likely to do so with beginners who traditionally tend to overstock their waters. The usual signs of oxygen deficiency will be the goldfish gasping at the surface for air. Unless the situation is rapidly corrected then the fish will suffocate and be found dead with their mouths open and their gill covers likewise.

The goldfish themselves are variable in their oxygen needs, dependent on both the temperature and on their individual metabolic rates. In warmer water they will be more active, as to be expected, but apart from this, two fish of the same size may require differing amounts of oxygen in order to perform the same muscular movements, this reflecting their internal efficiency as biological units.

Clearly, with so many factors to consider, it is virtually impossible to provide an environment that is ideally suited to all of the occupants, so it is a case of finding, by trial and error, that level which seems to satisfy the needs of the fish without upsetting the overall ecosystem they are in. With this in mind, the first consideration should be in ensuring that the oxygen content of the water is adequate to meet the needs of the goldfish and of beneficial bacteria that colonize the substrate or aquarium base.

Aeration systems provide extra oxygen not by direct input into the water itself but by creating water circulation and by agitation at the surface. In the unaerated container the oxygen will be richest at the surface but the midwater will be far less so and the base will contain little. We can change this situation by pumping air into the lower depths. This will create a circulating current that will take the lower waters to the surface and in turn the oxygen-rich upper waters will be drawn down to replace that which is moving up.

CIRCULATION

The benefits of having a good circulatory system are numerous and are not all concerned with aeration. A by-product of respiration is carbon dioxide and in excess this is dangerous to the goldfish. When water is circulated, the carbon dioxide is carried to the surface, and as its concentration in the water is greater than that of its concentration in the atmosphere, it is released to the latter—the exact reverse of the situation with

A rare mix: a blue-scale (silver coloration) goldfish with a fanned-out tail (butterfly) and telescope eyes. Photo: Fred Rosenzweig

A pearlscaled oranda. Photo: Bob Mertlich

oxygen, which is richer in the air than in the water. Other potentially harmful gases are likewise dissipated into the air by means of water circulation.

Unless water is moving, it will tend to form layers at differing temperatures, so by introducing an aerator we ensure that all the aquarium water remains at a constant heat. Circulation is also vital to healthy plant growth because it carries needed minerals to the plants which are required for their growth. It also removes unwanted by-products of their metabolism, and this includes excess oxygen which the circulation thus carries around the aquarium for the benefit of the other inhabitants.

SIMPLE AERATION

The most popular means of providing aeration to an aquarium is via an airstone attached to an air line. The airstone is placed on the substrate at the rear of the tank—where it can be discreetly hidden—

and it generates a constant stream of bubbles which draw water to the surface with them as they rise. Beginners often think that the bubbles themselves are the source of the oxygenation of the water but this is not actually so, or not so in simple airstones. Of all the hundreds of bubbles that are seen rising, very few of them will actually burst before they reach the surface, so they account for a negligible amount of added oxygen. Their effect is related to the fact that they take deoxygenated water from the lower levels to the surface where it is re-charged with this gas before being taken back down in the circulatory current.

Most airstones are made of porous inert materials and the size of the holes in them will determine the size of the bubbles. The smaller these are, the greater the chance they will burst before reaching the surface. The more expensive air stones are long and can create a decorative curtain of bubbles at the rear of the tank. In such cases they not only increase the amount of oxygen in the water by the extra agitation but can actually make a reasonable contribution to oxygen directly in the water due to their sheer numbers. Although most aquariums of small size feature only one airstone, it is better if two are used, one on each side of the tank. This will provide a better and more even circulation of the water as well as increasing the oxygen potential.

AIR PUMPS

The pumps available today for both air and water circulation come in a very extensive range of potential outputs and prices. Those that provide air are

In the ryukin, red markings increase as the fish ages. A year before this photo was taken, this fish was completely white. Photo: Fred Rosenzweig

graded according to the amount of cubic centimeters they can produce per minute and all those to be seen in your pet or aquatic store will have sufficient capacity to meet the needs of a small aquarium. They are produced to a remarkably high level of reliability and the noise level associated with vibrator diaphragm type pumps has, to a large extent, been eliminated in the latest models. These latter pumps are the more popular, though piston models are still available and have a strong following with the more dedicated enthusiasts who want long life and silent, powerful capacity.

Regular partial changes of the water in an aquarium are of great benefit to the fishes. Such changes can be made with siphons and buckets, or in a more labor-saving manner through the use of water-changing equipment available at pet shops. Photo courtesy of Aquarium Products

When first setting up an aquarium there is little point in purchasing a very powerful pump for its own sake, so you are advised to discuss the choice with your supplier and with reference to the size of the aquarium you plan to purchase. Given that most pumps will have the needed out-

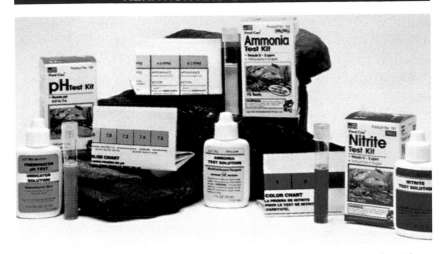

Testing of the water destined for use in garden ponds for its ammonia and nitrite levels as well as its pH and hardness has been made much easier for hobbyists because of the introduction of test kits that are reliable and easy to use. Photo courtesy of Aquarium Pharmaceuticals

put, then the other considerations you will be interested in will be the electric current used, the noise level, whether the pump has one or two outlets (probably only one on pumps up to about 2000 cc min) and if the spare parts situation is good (a friend using a similar pump is more likely to be able to comment without bias on this latter aspect). The better models will normally have adjustable control knobs on them but if not, then air clamps can be used to regulate the supply of air. The larger units will be more efficient and deliver more air at a cheaper cost but the current used by any pump is negligible. Minor servicing needs of vibrator pumps can be attended to by the average handy person and it is worthwhile purchasing a few spare parts when you buy the pump; in some cases these will be part of the package. When siting the pump, consideration must be given to the fact that if it is below the water surface level, then if it is switched off, or if there is a power failure, the water in the tank can back-siphon and enter the pump where it will do much damage in all probability—apart from flooding the immediate area. To avoid this, a non-return valve should be placed along the airline length, or a non-siphon bend should be a feature of the air line. This can be plastic tubing which is an inverted 'U' where it leaves the aquarium. Alternatively, the pump should be placed at least 15cm (6in) above the water level—possibly suspended, which will reduce even further any drumming noise resulting from the vibration of the pump.

Should a piston pump be purchased, this will require periodic oiling, and it is very important to ensure that no oil gains access to the airline, as it is dangerous to the health of your fish. Such pumps must always be specifi-

Laying out a complicated array of ponds connected by flowing water can be difficult unless everything is perfectly level.

Partitioning a pond sometimes works, but often it is more trouble than it is worth. It is better to keep only compatible fishes and have emergency aquariums for treatment of diseased specimens.

cally designed for aquarium use and should only be purchased from pet shops or aquatic dealers who understand these aspects; always give your business to those who can also provide you with service and advice whenever you run into problems.

Once a pump is set up and running, it should be left in that state and not switched off at night, because this is very bad for the overall aquatic environment. Temperatures will fluctuate more readi-ly and the drop in oxygen content of the water will adversely affect all the inhabitants. If plants are included, over night they will be consuming oxygen and releasing carbon dioxide, so this is the very time the pump should be operating—the saving on electricity you can forget, because you could not calculate such a minor amount in your overall consumption. Periodically you will need to clean the filter of the pump, but such servicing will take only a short while—otherwise the golden rule is to keep all aquatic systems operating round the clock. The only equipment that should be turned off at night is the aquarium lighting.

When discussing aeration, it must be stated that it is important that the substrate be oxygenated as well as the water above it. If this is not done, it will be unable to support beneficial bacteria and as a result organic waste will decompose and release harmful compounds and gases into the water. To achieve such aeration, aquarists combine this with a method of filtration. For those planning to keep their goldfish in a pond, the addition of oxygen via air pumps is not needed, because it will be provided during the filtration process; this is equally as true in aquariums, but in those latter containers one sometimes sees aeration being achieved independent of filtration, though this is not usually required.

An aquarium that is well aerated and filtered can in fact contain a substantially larger number of fish than its surface area would suggest, but one must understand the risks one takes when using aeration to increase stock levels. If the power source should fail for any length of time, the fish will rapidly find life unbearable and a number might suffocate. Goldfish, along with other species, regulate their growth rate in relation to the water space they live in; thus it follows that in an overstocked aquarium they will never attain potential maximum growth.

Aeration should be applied sensibly in terms of stock levels so that one can have a few more fish, provided the aquarium is of reasonable size to start with, but the main function of adding oxygen is basically to ensure there is a sufficient quantity to meet the needs of the goldfish, the plants, and all other air-breathing organisms essential to a balanced biological environment. A final point on the subject of aeration is that goldfish evolved in slow-moving waters—as did many of the plants. This means they are not happy in waters which buffet them about because the owner is determined to make sure there is no shortage of oxygen. Gentle aeration is therefore the required situation for the fish and for plants native to similar waters. Build up your stock levels slowly so that at no point are you suddenly changing the nature of the habitat in any dramatic way. Thus you will quickly come to appreciate when you are approaching the safe limits of a given aquarium size.

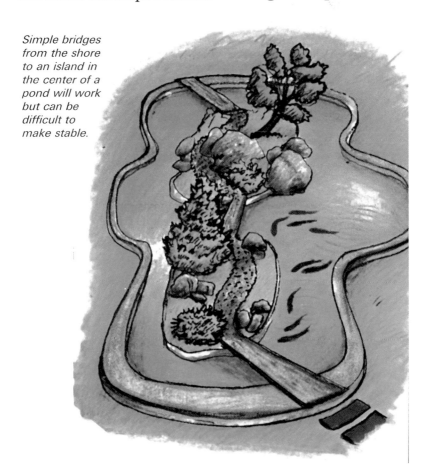

Simple bridges from the shore to an island in the center of a pond will work but can be difficult to make stable.

If you can't see them, you can't appreciate them.

Filtration

If an aquarium has good aeration, this fact alone will make life far better for the fish than if it does not. However, it hardly creates a workable eco-system, because it does not remove the many forms of debris and unwanted toxic chemicals from the water. In natural waters this is done in many ways, such as the current steadily carrying unwanted materials downstream. The considerable variety of other life forms also helps keep rivers and lakes clean, and of course the overall size of the water volume in relation to the size of the fish is such that the toxic properties it contains are held in only very minute traces which the fish can tolerate. An aquarium or pond is hardly comparable because it is so small and has no means of removing unwanted materials and chemicals, so we must organize this in much the same way as we have to do in our own homes.

The general cleansing process of a contained body of water is known as filtration in aquaculture even though only part of it is actually true filtration. In achieving good filtration we can, as a by-product, attain excellent aeration and water circulation; indeed, circulation is vital to filtration. There are many very complex filter systems available these days and fully understanding the more advanced types is a study in itself. However, in their basic principles they all do exactly the same thing as the very simplest forms, but just do it far better.

Exactly what filter system is employed should directly reflect the level of pollution to be found in an aquarium or pond. For example, if a tank is stocked with a large number of fish, it will require a more complex and powerful system than if it has only two goldfish in it. The object is always to relate the filter system to the amount of garbage, in its many forms, that the system is expected to cope with. The way it is achieved is basically to pump the aquarium water into one or more external containers in which are various filter media, and thence return the purified water back to the aquarium, aerating it at the same time. It is possible to have internal filters but these are not only less convenient to use but are really only practical in small volumes of water—where of course they take up valuable space and tend to be a bit of an eyesore. External filters can be conveniently hidden yet be such that they can easily be serviced.

A simple filter can be achieved by utilizing the air-lift system or it can be done via a power filter which actually circulates the water around and through filters as described above. The latter are clearly the best and can be used in the smallest of aquariums or in the very largest possible garden pond. In the average small home aquarium the filter box is conveniently hung on the side of the tank, but in more sophisticated arrangements the filter boxes are placed close by but separate from the aquarium or pond. Before looking at filter systems, let us discuss a few general aspects.

PUMPS

Even more than with air pumps, there are today many models of power filter pumps. Some incorporate

built-in filters while others purely move the water by impellers built into them much in the way a motor car pump operates. They are graded by the liters or gallons of water they can move in an hour (LPH or GPH). Because a water pump is a more complex piece of equipment it will cost more than an air pump and so more thought should go into its choice—especially where garden ponds or large aquariums are concerned. The size of pump required will be controlled by the volume of water your aquarium or pond, including the filter boxes, contains and the speed with which you wish it to circulate the entire volume. This of course will depend on the number of fish being kept and, in the case of outdoor ponds,

Aeration of the aquarium has come a long way from piston-driven pumps and wooden airstones. Today powerful pumps and filters produce excellent filtering with increased aeration all in one step. Use of modern equipment requires that you carefully follow all manufacturer's instructions, however.

Goldfish are peaceful fish that can tolerate a broad variety of water conditions, including marginally warm waters. This platy and swordtail tank could house a few small goldfish, at least for a while. Note the extensive use of plastic plants and the curtain of bubbles produced by the bubble wand aerator.

the time of the year. In the latter you want only a slow circulation overwinter whereas you need a high water movement during the summer—both to cool the pond and to cope with the much greater level of pollution found at this very active period. When viewing water pumps, consider wheth- er they have the facility to take extra equipment, such as suction pipes for cleaning; pipes for water- falls or similar installa- tion in the case of ponds. Also, where the latter are concerned you should try and establish their fall- off rate when applied to lifting water. Two simi- lar-output pumps at a

An internal power filter can be put right into the tank, with both pump and filtering areas being completely submerged. Photo courtesy of Penn Plax

given head of water (the height the water is lifted) can differ considerably as this increases.

Pumps for garden ponds are certainly the more complex to consider because if you plan to feature a waterfall and a fountain, the pump will need a very powerful capacity. A waterfall will need approximately 300 gallons per hour in order to exhibit a continual flow over just 15cm (6in) and that is not a very high waterfall. If the pump's capacity was only 400 gph clearly you would have problems if the waterfall was not to be fed independent of the filtration system.

As a general rule, I would recommend that you always purchase a water pump that has a greater capacity than what you think you will need. This is because it is probable you will add extra equipment on the one hand, and may well purchase a larger aquarium at a later date on the other hand. Also, you do not want to have your pump operating at maximum output all of the time but rather have it working nicely within its capabilities. Another consideration for pond owners is that the pump is designed to take the size of water piping you plan to use in your circulation. This, again, behooves you to purchase your pump from a pet shop or aquatic dealer who can advise you on your whole system so that it is integrated and balanced to give you the performance you will come to expect of it. In many aquatic stores you will

The finnage of some goldfish, such as this broadtail telescope, is very delicate and reacts to increased ammonia levels by developing red blood spots in some areas. Photo: Fred Rosenzweig

have the opportunity of seeing various pumps in action in display tanks, and these will give you a good idea of how efficient they are.

EXTRACTED MATERIALS

An aspect of filtration that is sometimes not appreciated by novice owners is that the full process is not completed by the removal of toxic chemicals from the water and into the filter box. Indeed, if filters are left uncleaned, they will actually perpetuate the very condition you are trying to avoid because they will eventually discharge the pollutants back into the aquarium and this will reduce what is known as the redox potential (the ability to absorb oxygen). When this happens, the water may well appear clear, but its toxic prop-

A pearl toad-head, a type of bubble-eye with poorly developed bubbles. Such fish are generally weak and will not do well in pond conditions. Photo: Tom Caravaglia

An interesting pair of lionheads. Lionheads often are confused with orandas, but they lack the dorsal fin. Photo: Burkhard Kahl

erties will be rising and as this happens, the water's ability to hold oxygen will actually fall and no amount of aeration will improve this negative cycle. This being so, filtration is really achieved only once the unwanted debris and chemicals are removed from the filter boxes, which must be serviced on a regular basis with this in mind. Cou-pled with this is the need to make regular checks on the water condition so that nothing escapes your attention. These routine chores take very little time at all, yet are vital to sound husbandry.

PRE-FILTER CONSIDERATIONS

In order that the filter system proper is not over-loaded and clogged up, any accumulations of large debris should be removed before the water enters the filter. This can be done manually with a siphon used on the substrate. Pond owners can purchase special vacuum attachments for their water pumps to achieve this state. In the case of ponds, it is useful to include a bottom drain in order to remove silt that gathers at the bottom. In both aquariums and ponds it is beneficial that the base has a slope to it in order that mulm is drawn down to a convenient point. In the aquarium, this is achieved by sloping the gravel to the front of the tank; in the pond, the actual base of this has an incline on it either to the drains or to a point that can be cleaned by siphon tools. Algae should be periodically scraped from aquariums so that it does not eventually clog the filters.

In a pond (and even in a large aquarium setup), a settlement box can be installed and the idea of this is that water is pumped into this box before it enters the filter boxes. Sediment of large size sinks to the bottom where it can be removed on a regular basis. Most power filters will have a strainer pre-filter built into them and this should be routinely cleaned or replaced.

FILTER MEDIA

There are basically two types of unwanted material to be found in a body of contained water. These are, firstly, that material which is small enough to pass through pre-filters, and secondly, that which will pass through any filter medium, that is, it is soluble in water, such as gases and numerous chemical compounds. Filters are therefore classed according to the function they perform and may be grouped as follows:

1. Mechanical filters. These remove materials from the water by straining them out. At the point

Goldfish can develop to their finest only in water that is relatively free of growth-retarding nitrogenous compounds that could be removed by efficient filtration. Photo by Fred Rosenzweig.

they are trapped, they can be removed.

2. Chemical filters. These either absorb chemicals or render them harmless by combining chemically with them to produce a new compound that is not injurious to the fish.

3. Biological filters. These are also chemical filters in that they break down compounds that are dangerous and convert them into less toxic substances which either dissipate into the atmosphere as gases or are absorbed by plants and animals as nutrients.

In reality, a number of filter media perform a double role, as they may act as both mechanical and biological strainers. One cannot identify any one filter medium as being more important than another, because much will depend on the nature of that which is to be removed. For example, if an aquarium has only a small number of tiny goldfish in it, there will be much less organic matter to be processed—but the level of dirt in the water might be such that the mechanical filter is the most needed. In another aquarium the need may be for chemical filtration and so on, thus a filter system should be all-embracing but may be biased one way or another in keeping with the conditions in the particular aquarium in question. No two volumes of water are ever quite the same, so their filtration needs must be on an individual basis; in a pond this will also be seasonal.

MECHANICAL FILTERS

Any material that will prevent particles of dirt from passing through it but allow the water to proceed onwards is a potential mechanical filter medium. How effective it is will be determined by the size of the holes in it or by its density. For example, plastic mesh comes in many grades of hole size, so the choice will reflect

An interesting and attractive pair of Chinese calico lionheads. Photo: Fred Rosenzweig

the size of the debris to be filtered. Likewise, this is true of nylon wool, which is even more effective than meshing. However, if its density is too great, it will quickly become a less suitable medium not because it fails to do its job but because its interfilamentary spaces quickly become filled and thus restrict the movement of the water itself. Fine sand is a good mechanical filter, but its density renders it less useful unless under considerable pressure. Gravel is a good mechanical filter providing, again, it is not too fine, but it should be very hard stone—not any that will erode and merely add to the chemical toxics in the water. Foam is yet another favored filter, but care should be taken to ensure that this is prepared for aquatic use, as many foams (and nylon wool) used for domestic purposes (furniture padding and such) may contain toxic properties if immersed in water. Another very good filter medium is a series of small nylon brushes. These are gaining popularity in pond filter systems; they are specially made for aquatic use and available from good aquatic stores.

CHEMICAL FILTERS

The most popular chemical filter for aquarists is activated carbon. It has a very large surface area compared to its size and this is due to its porous nature. Dissolved chemicals in the water are absorbed by it. It has a definite use period after which it fails to adsorb further and at such times must be replaced. Its activity can be tested by placing methylene blue in a test tube containing some of the carbon and then adding water. If the carbon is still charged, the water will become clear—if it remains blue then the carbon is no longer absorbing. The

quality of a given carbon can be likewise tested, for charcoal varies in its adsorption powers.

Zeolite is another useful chemical filter that has the advantage that it can be cleaned when its absorbing powers are waning. Simply soak it for 24 hours in a concentrated salt solution, dry, and it is ready for use again. Do remember, however, that if salt is used in the aquarium as a general tonic for the water, zeolite's use is neutralized and any ammonia or similar chemicals it has absorbed will be released back into the water. Likewise, carbon will adsorb medicaments added to an aquarium and in so doing may release toxins they are charged with. With this fact in mind, both carbon and zeolite should be removed from filters if a tank is to be treated with medicines.

Both of these chemical filters do, of course, act as mechanical filters and may even become biological filters as well because their

Goldfish have been bred for at least 500 years, probably much longer, so they have developed more varieties than any other domesticated fish. Often only an expert can provide the proper name for a fish, and experts often disagree among themselves. Photo: Burkhard Kahl

surface area provides a good home for aerobic bacteria. However, this latter function would restrict your ability to clean them properly. Some aquarists advocate leaving spent carbon in the aquarium to function as a biological fil-ter, but this carries the risk that the carbon might release toxic chemicals it has absorbed, so this is not a practice I would recommend. It is possible to use ion exchange resins in the aquarium as chemical filters but this should not be necessary in a well-balanced aquarium and is not without certain risks. When chemical filters are excessively used, they can totally change the overall composition of water and may remove valuable trace elements which are beneficial to water quality. Most aquarists are far more aware of what properties water should not have than what it should, and, as a result, in attempting to remove potentially harmful material we may well be doing likewise to valuable compounds, so moderation is the best order of the day.

BIOLOGICAL FILTERS

There are both plant and bacterial biological filters. In the case of the former, they are any plants that are placed into the aquarium. They absorb many chemical compounds as nutrients and a number of these would ordinarily be harmful to the fish such as nitrates or ammonia. Bacterial biological filters are minute bacteria which convert ammonia to nitrites; other bacteria convert the nitrites to nitrates which the plants then partially absorb. To be effective, aerobic bacteria filters must have a constant oxygen supply around them and as the bacteria are mostly found on the substrate, it is essential that this is kept free of mulm accumulations. This is best done with gravel siphon cleaners purchased from petshops, or by regular siphoning.

AQUATIC BALANCE

The problem confronting all aquarists is that in attaining a satisfactory level of water condition for the fish, it may not be as acceptable to other inhabitants whose contribution to the ecosystem is nonetheless of benefit to the fish. In open natural waters, this problem is not seen because of the constant flow situation, large surface area, rain, drainage through the substrate and so on. We are concerned about attaining a

A truly attractive red and white oranda. Bright colors, especially red, are among the goldfish's many attractions. Photo: Fred Rosenzweig

good level of water clarity, and this necessitates removing useful as well as negative properties—but these negatives are only so because we deem them as such. The anaerobic bacteria, and dirt itself, are part of a natural system that is balanced because of the large volumes involved.

As an example, the presence of green algae in the water is a healthy sign because these simple plants require a high level of free oxygen. However, a number of aquatic plants from slow-moving rivers prefer a reduced oxygen level, and even microorganisms that assist in the breakdown of toxic properties do not all prefer high oxygen levels or water that is constantly moving—but others do. It becomes impossible to satisfy all needs in a container as small as an aquarium—and even a very large tank is still a relatively small volume of water. We can test water for pH value, hardness, nitrate content, copper levels, and so on, but even when all of this is done, it is actually only the tip of the iceberg and there is still a great deal we do not understand about balancing water habitats. Hydrologists—those who study water and its cycles—are continually coming up with new information that we previously did not understand. As a result, the more we treat water with filters and chemicals, the more it becomes apparent that our efforts, while achieving short-term success, may actually create longer-term problems for the fish. The chemical equilibrium in the water between the various ions becomes distorted to a degree we cannot see or test for in any simple manner.

No organisms can survive in totally pure water for long before it starts to adversely affect their well-being. The only way we become aware that apparently super conditions are not really so great is when our fish start to keel over and die. This tends to be a sudden happening and takes us by surprise—plants may be a better indicator of water condition, especially if they are native to similar waters to the fish. Conversely, if plants are placed in an aquarium substrate that are known to prefer well-oxygenated waters, then their failure to prosper will be a sign that the substrate has too low a redox potential.

Keeping goldfish in an aquarium is thus always a compromise situation between various factors, and these factors change daily. In order that we reduce the risk that filtration systems move the unseen water condition too far one way or the other, it is essential that a given volume of

A six-year-old Chinese lionhead of excellent quality. Notice how the head growth is thicker than the width of the body. Photo: Fred Rosenzweig

the water is removed periodically. In so doing, we are at least sure that a reasonable degree of neutrality is being introduced into the overall system. It is a reasonably reliable constant so should be included in any of our strategies.

FILTER SYSTEMS

A filter system may be a simple foam material placed in the path of an air lift or it may be a complex series of chambers or containers each having its own filter medium—as are seen in many large garden ponds. Highly complex units are beyond the scope of this book because the average goldfish owner, whether keeping an aquarium or a pond, is unlikely to be thinking in terms of high numbers of tanks or a vast pond. In any case, it happens that the principles applied are the same, and many an aquarist with a basic system that is well balanced has achieved better success than another whose complex system creates its own problems of balance.

AIR LIFT FILTER

If an air stone is placed into a tube which has its bottom end inserted into a plastic container packed with nylon wool, and which also has holes in its sides, this will act as a very simple mechanical filter. The rising air stream is lighter than the surrounding water, so the latter is lifted up the tube and in so doing draws water in through the nylon wool container which thus traps particles of dirt in it which can be periodically removed.

Carbon could be placed on top of the nylon wool, thus providing chemical filtration as well. Such a small system is clearly lim-

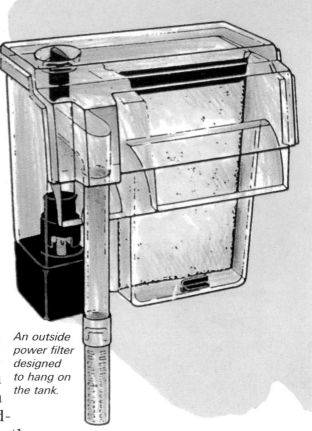

An outside power filter designed to hang on the tank.

ited in its ability to filter, but nonetheless in a small aquarium is better than nothing. There are numerous variations on this principle.

Facing page: Top: A mixed-breed bubble-eyed oranda with long finnage. Photo: Fred Rosenzweig Bottom: A top U.S.-bred ranchu. Although still white at six months of age, the fins will later pick up red markings. Photo: Fred Rosenzweig

A pearlscale goldfish showing the
characteristic swollen scales.
Photo: Andre Roth

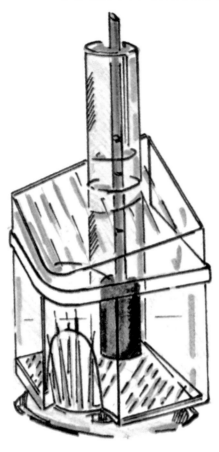

A corner filter comes in handy in small aquariums such as quarantine tanks.

EXTERNAL AIRLIFT FILTERS

Somewhat better is an air lift external box filter. This hangs on the side of the aquarium and in it is placed nylon wool, foam, and charcoal—or whatever filter medium is decided upon. A siphon action draws water from the aquarium into the filter box where it is sucked down through the filters and enters a tube containing the air stone, which provides the upward current to return it to the aquarium. The siphon should draw water from the bottom of the tank, just above the substrate, and it will need priming to set the circulation in motion. Place the siphon tube into the aquarium so it fills with water, then cap this with your finger or a bung and take one end to the filter box; once you release your finger, the water will flow and continue to do so until the filter box is full to the same level as the tank. In the event that the air lift should fail to operate, the filter box will not flood, because it will only fill until it reaches the level as mentioned when the siphon will stop. Of course, the box must be positioned so that its sides are higher than the aquarium water level. These are inexpensive filters that are easily

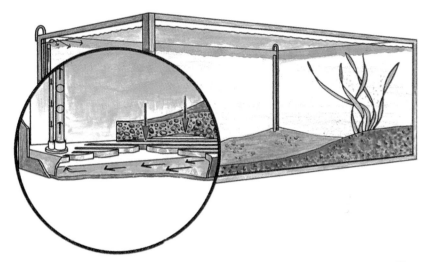

The workings of a typical undergravel filter are shown in the inset circle. The bubbles rising in the air lift tube, operated by the pump, cause a partial vacuum that helps pull tank water through the gravel to be circulated through the air lift or riser tubes. The gravel serves as both a cleansing medium to remove dirt and a substrate for nitrogen cycle bacteria.

serviced and quiet in action. They provide gentle filtration but are not especially suited to the larger aquarium where their action is rather slow to be really efficient.

UNDERGRAVEL FILTERS

The advantage of an undergravel filter is that it deals very effectively with ammonia and its compounds—those produced by feces, urine, and the bacterial breakdown of organic food and other waste. No filter medium is needed, as the system utilizes the aerobic bacteria that live in and on the substrate. However, a filter plate must be incorporated into the tank when it is initially set up. The plate is raised from the base of the tank and has many small holes in it which allow water to pass through it. Above the plate the substrate is placed. An air lift tube is featured at one comer of the plate and inside this is the air tube

Many aquarists feel that an undergravel filter is not best for planted tanks, as the constant circulation of water through the roots of the plants causes poor growth. Other aquarists disagree. Of course, many goldfish keepers get around the problem by using plastic plants.

itself, attached to the diffuser stone.

The rising stream of air bubbles and water draws water down through the substrate and thence into the air lift, which returns it to the water surface. The object is to create a good supply of well oxygenated water in the substrate, thus encouraging the colonies of aerobic bacteria to build up in order to offset the negatives of anaerobic bacteria with their ammo-nium-producing features. The system is silent and hidden away under the gravel and will last for a long period of time before it needs cleaning. It can be improved by fitting a power head to the air lift, which will speed up the whole water circulation and increase the aeration of the water by the disturbance at the surface.

However, such biological filters do have inherent disadvantages that must be overcome. Firstly, they encourage dirt and decaying matter to enter the substrate and secondly, the turbulence in the substrate may not be appreciated by rooted plants, which may have difficulty in both anchoring themselves and in gaining nutrients from the water. If one does not keep the substrate clean, then the benefits of the system will be largely negated because the gravel will clog. Thus there will be a buildup of anaerobic bacteria which will feed on the aerobic organisms which will be killed by the lack of oxygen in the substrate. The filter plate should cover the entire aquarium base.

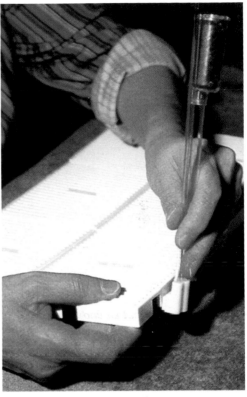

Inserting an airlift or riser tube into the appropriate slot of an undergravel filter. This tube is equipped with a cylinder of activated carbon, which helps remove some dissolved chemical impurities.

Such filters can be made more efficient by the use of water pumps which will increase the speed of the operation and which can pass the water through conventional mechanical and chemicals filters before sending it back into the aquarium. A further variation which has considerable advantage is to send the water in the opposite direction, this being known as reverse flow filtration. Here water is

Common ryukin goldfish of plain silvery coloration. Except for the higher body, they resemble wild goldfish. Photo: Midori Shobo

then returned to the aquarium under the filter plate. Thus it does not draw debris into the substrate, which is also supplied with filtered water in the first place. It provides well-aerated water to the lower levels of the aquarium. It is argued that this is an unnatural system because of the reverse flow and that such systems will require extra aeration by one or other means. However, an aquarium is an unnatural system anyway, so that objection has little merit, and reverse flow is certainly more efficient if viewed in terms of its ability to cope with ammonium by-products—again it is a case of compromise and personal preferences. It is essential that in undergravel filters the seals to the air lift are good and that no areas of the tank are left so that anaerobic bacteria drawn from just above the substrate and passed through an external filter or a canister filter. It is

A very nice and colorful ryukin with a trace of bubble-eye ancestry. The color is the epitome of a true "goldfish." Photo: Burkhard Kahl

can develop isolated colonies, for these would counteract the otherwise numerous advantages of this form of filtration. It can be mentioned that on a more massive scale this same system can be used in garden ponds; it is advised that about two-thirds of the pond base should be covered by the undergravel filter. The results of such a system are excellent and provide trouble-free maintenance coupled with good water clarity—but such a system will need incorporating at the design stage because of the extra depth required to accommodate it.

Common comet goldfish are attractive in their own way, though certainly not fancy. They often are used as food for other fishes. Photo: Michael Gilroy

POWER FILTERS

The singular advantage of a power filter is that it can circulate the water around an aquarium at a much faster pace and, in so doing, can also be used to increase aeration. The simplest power filters are of the hand-on box type mentioned already. They work on the same basis but of course no airlift action is needed, because the water is circulated by a motor fixed into the box filter chamber.

More sophisticated are the canister models which have filters built into them. They come in an extensive range and can be situated away from the aquarium. The filtered water can be returned by a power spray or via spray bars. These are lengths of plastic tubing attached to the rear of the tank via suction pads, and they are perforated along their length with small holes. This provides excellent water-to-air interchange as well as creating turbulence at the actual aquarium surface.

As a general guide it is best to purchase a power filter that can pump the total aquarium volume about twice per hour—so a 30-gallon aquarium should use a pump with a gph capacity of 60 gallons. The actual rate you choose to circulate the water will reflect the need based on number of fish and so on.

OTHER FILTER SYSTEMS

The systems so far discussed are all available from your aquatic supplier, but of course it is quite possible for you to devise your own system using the principles outlined and making use of the power pumps now available. For example, goldfish are pretty rough in their treatment of plants, but you can still enjoy the benefits and beauty of plants by featuring them in a separate aquarium sited next to the goldfish home. You simply link the two tanks to each other via either a siphon tube or by pumping the water from one to the other (draw from the goldfish tank and return the filtered water from the biological tank). In such instances you can include other inmates that ordinarily would not be advised in a goldfish aquarium, such as various snail species. You can cultivate *Daphnia* in a biological tank and this will provide a

Diatom filters are useful for periodic cleaning of tanks and even small ponds.

ready source of live food for your fish. Another benefit is that you can disconnect the two tanks should you wish to add medicaments to the goldfish aquarium. Such a biotank could supply two goldfish units, so this is an interesting yet efficient variation.

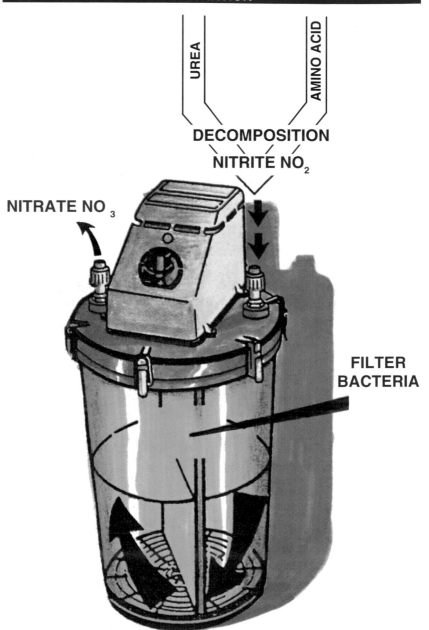

UREA

AMINO ACID

DECOMPOSITION

NITRITE NO$_2$

NITRATE NO$_3$

FILTER BACTERIA

A greatly simplified diagram of the working of a canister filter and its nitrogen cycle bacteria.

POND FILTRATION

The only difference between a goldfish aquarium and a pond is one of size—plus the fact that the latter is open to the elements in most cases (but it is possible to have an indoor pond). This being so, filtration methods are the same but on a larger scale. It is also more advisable to have two or even three separate filter chambers each performing a specific function. Air lift systems are not practical in ponds, so it is all accomplished by power equipment, and aeration is included within the filter systems, being returned via sprays, fountains, or waterfalls.

In this book as a whole, I have avoided quoting chemical reactions via formulas because the average person just about to commence keeping goldfish has enough to absorb in terms of basic principles. However, those disposed toward chemistry or with a higher than normal interest in limnology (the study of inland waters and their make-up) are advised to purchase a book specifically on water chemistry which will provide far more detail than will be found in a book covering aquatics as a general subject. However, I do stress that a chemical knowledge is by no means essential to successful aquaculture, which is more concerned with one's ability to appreciate fundamental aquatic principles and general management techniques and routine.

UTILIZE YOUR DEALER

It is hoped that the reader will appreciate that keeping goldfish is in fact more involved than simply filling up an aquarium with water. It need not be a scientific operation, but you will certainly benefit from investing in the equipment mentioned. With this in mind, and the likely problems you may encounter along the years, it makes very good sense to cash in on an aquatic dealer's vast experience.

Above: *Diagram of the theory behind an open filter bed or trickle filter. Overflow water from the aquarium flows down through the large pipe and through a filter bed in a separate tank. The cleansed water is returned to the aquarium by a pump.*

This water pump-operated fountain provides aeration and a certain amount of water movement in addition to the good looks and feeling of serenity it provides. Photo by Michael Gilroy

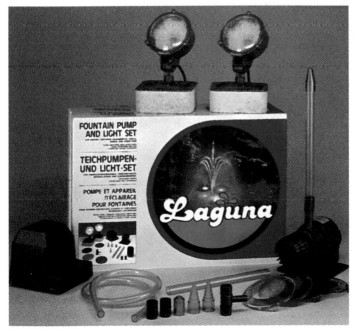

Kits that contain lights as well as fountain-like aeration equipment can be obtained at pet shops and tropical fish specialty stores.

Aquarium lighting recently has had a revolution with many new types becoming available for special purposes. Unfortunately, many of the more specialized lights are very expensive to purchase and opeate.

Lighting

Lighting is used in aquariums for two basic reasons, the most important of which, from a biological viewpoint, is to encourage the growth of plants. The other reason is to highlight the fish, in which case the light is purely decorative. We have already discussed the fact that natural sunlight has serious disadvantages for aquarists because it cannot be controlled easily, nor can it be relied upon to be reliably present in all places. Further, the fact that it enters the tank mainly from the side can distort the way the plants grow and indeed the angle at which the goldfish swim. This means that aquarium lighting is better supplied by artificial sources. There is today quite a range of these to suit all needs; some are, however, much more appropri-

A hanging or pendant metal halide light used to help algae grow. Such lights often are of use when culturing young fishes.

ate to the coldwater aquarium than are others.

TYPES OF LIGHTING

There are basically four types of lighting used in aquaculture at this time and these are tungsten, spotlights, high pressure mercury lamps and fluorescent tubes. Of these, the first and last are suited to the average aquarium. Spotlights provide penetrating light, which is fine for the deep aquarium, but they generate much heat and are not practical to fit, being too bulky for hoods; they are also expensive to run. Mercury lamps, together with metal halide and sodium lamps, also emit considerable light that is useful in the deep aquarium, but they must be suspended about 30 cm (12 in) above the tank and cannot be used in conjunction with normal hoods. Again, they generate much heat.

GARDEN PONDS

Lighting in garden ponds is purely decorative, as natural daylight obviously meets the needs of plants and others in the biosystem of the pond. However, the same rules of safety should be applied to the electrical supply. Ensure all wiring to ponds is very well insulated and if buried in the ground then make this at least 45cm (18in) deep so you are unlikely to accidentally spade into the wiring. You should also draw up a plan of exactly where any buried cables lie, and this should be made available to new owners should you sell your house.

There are numerous lights available for in-pond use, but do check that they really are for such use and have an electrician install them for you. Lighting can also be supplied to fountains and it is possible these days to have color-changing filters fitted to lights to produce interesting sequences to waterfall or fountain illumination. Any wiring near your pond should be protected by a circuit breaker which will trip everything off the moment there is any leak of current. Do make sure

The intricacies of judging the head growths of orandas and lionheads are too complex for any but the most advanced hobbyists. This Chinese lionhead has the massive body appreciated in the breed and also has a heavy and well-developed head growth. Photo: Fred Rosenzweig

such a breaker is in fact covering all wiring and not just one plug. Many pond appliances utilize reduced voltage in conjunction with a transformer, and these are useful in reducing the risk of danger from electric shocks.

The great danger that can be posed by electrical equipment and connections in proximity to water is just one reason why your electrically powered pool equipment should always be from reliable manufacturers.

Plants

PLANTS AS DECORATION

Vegetation provides excellent decoration in an aquarium, for rarely does an unplanted aquascene look complete. The plants can be divided into a few basic groups according to their use in decorative terms. There are floating plants which have leaves on the surface and may flower; there are bunch or filler plants that are seen at their best in groups used in the middle ground of the aquarium, and there are foreground plants which are obviously smaller. Finally, there are specimen plants which are used anywhere in the tank (though usually in the foreground) and act as a focal point, so they are used as a single plant or maybe just two or three.

Apart from decoration, plants are important in an aquarium for the shelter they provide for the fish, as

This calico oranda has excellent head growth for the breed. Head growth reflects not only age but also genetics and water conditions to some extent. Photo: Fred Rosenzweig

a potential spawning medium, and, of course, as a food source. It is this latter aspect that worries many beginners but as long as there is a good ratio of plants to fish, and the fish are fed on good wholesome foods, then the damage done by goldfish is not really so bad at all. What is essential is that the plants must be well established, so young plantings must

Decorative plants in the garden pool can be put in containers or simply planted and allowed to spread as in the example shown here. In cool climates many plants (including water lilies) have to be taken in during the winter, which is easier to accomplish if plants are put into containers. Photo: P. Hodgkinson.

An interesting array of water lilies and other plants with floating leaves restricted to one corner of the pond and seeming to spread from a common center. Photo: Dr. Herbert R. Axelrod

be afforded some protection via pots or even by being screened with a fine plastic mesh until they have put on some growth. If you find, in spite of all your efforts, that a given plant does not succeed in your aquarium, but you wish to include it, then this is the occasion when a really good quality artificial plant could be used.

ACQUIRING PLANTS

Let me say straightaway that you are not advised to acquire plants for either the aquarium or pond from wild habitats. There will be the obvious risk that they will carry disease and most certainly will harbor unwanted insects in one or another of their life stages. The savings, taking into account your time and costs in gathering them, are really not worth the effort. It is much better to purchase from an aquatic specialist who will not only have healthy plants but will also have a good range of them, and of growing aids and utensils now available. Once the initial plants are purchased, you will be able to cultivate many of them in the manner to be discussed. Most plants suited to the coldwater aquarium, and which can survive the attentions of goldfish, are strong growers and not expensive to purchase.

PROPAGATION

Plants reproduce both sexually and asexually, the latter being known as vegetative reproduction. Plants flower when they generate male and female gametes, which allows for genetic exchange with other plants in order to maintain vigor. Asexual reproduction enables them to spread rapidly, so the two methods will often run in cycles.

Specialist aquatic hydroculturists utilize both methods, but most of us need only concern ourselves with vegetative reproduction—we are not looking to produce flowering heads on our aquarium plants. Here we can consider three methods of propagation which are very common. Should you see a plant in your dealer's shop that is not covered in this text, the dealer will tell you which of the methods is most suitable for propagating it. Pond plants are beyond the scope of this book. Those wanting further information on them are advised to purchase one of the titles published by TFH which are devoted to water plants. *Aquarium Plants*, by Rataj and Horeman (TFH style H-966) is especially recommended.

RUNNERS

These are modified stolons, which are branches that plants send out from their stems. These branches may travel across the substrate surface or below it. At intervals they will generate roots and then the stem will grow vertically, thus forming a new plant. In due course the plantlet will detach itself from the parent and will itself send out one or more runners. These offshoots can travel considerable distances before they put down roots, or they may develop quite near the mother plant, in which case they are termed offsets. Division is a simple case of detaching the plantlet from its parent stock and planting it into the desired position. Do not detach young plants too early, but wait until they have established themselves and are clearly growing nicely.

A shallow ledge in an informal garden pool provides plenty of room to put a variety of plants. In some areas, however, such a shallow and stagnant area would rapidly become a breeding ground for mosquitoes. Photo: Michael Gilroy

RHIZOMES

These are underground stems and not roots as might be thought; they are relatively thick because they act as food storage organs for the plant. They sprout leaves and buds and are propagated simply by cutting them into two or more pieces, each of which should then establish itself. In all cases where cutting is involved you can purchase compounds to dress, thus protect, the cut edges. Rhizomes are perennials but other swollen stems, such as corms and tubers, are annuals, so you cannot cut these. They will sprout another plant, and as this grows the parent plant will die back.

PLANTING

Whether you plant your aquarium when it is dry or

Interesting coloration and markings on a red and white oranda. The caudal finnage is excellent—long, with little indentation. The lobes are round and thick. A deep round body and good head growth complete the pleasing appearance. Photo: Fred Rosenzweig

when it is partially filled with water is not important, this being a personal view. In general, you get a better idea of the finished effect if the aquarium is partly filled so that the plant foliage rises; you will also be more sure that the plants are well anchored in the substrate. Once you are familiar with the plants, then you will know what they will look like, so dry planting is not then a problem. When anchoring plants, you can place cotton or lead weights around them (the cotton being attached to the lead or to special pot weights), but be careful that whatever binds them is not too tight. Pond plants can be placed into polyethylene bags containing numerous holes. In this way the compost is more readily retained and they can be lifted at the end of the season. The holes allow the roots to spread out as the plant

Facing page: *A suggested arrangement of aquatic plants for a small pond. This many plants put into too small a pond, however, could rapidly spread to cover the entire surface, making the fish invisible.*

Above: *Many backyard ponds are planned with shallow shelves around the edge intended to serve as home to bog and marsh plants that show emergent growth. Plants with a more submersed growth are put in the deeper sections of the pond.*

grows. Plastic pots also have such holes, so there are lots of choices.

Always ensure that plants have a growing tip above the substrate, especially with rhizomes and other swollen stems. Initially, a plant that is transferred from one habitat to another, such as from a dealer's tank to your own, will probably lose a number of its leaves. Do not assume it is dying, for new foliage should soon start to appear. Always prune plants of any dying leaves; otherwise these will fall to the aquarium substrate and decompose, adding to the production of ammonium compounds.

Avoid purchasing any plants that appear to be wilting, as this is a sure sign they are not receiving correct attention, so it is likely they will fail to make good their losses when you transfer them to your aquarium.

Plants will vary in the space they require, but as a general guide allow 26cm^2 (4in^2) for each plant in a coldwater aquarium. This is thus 36 plants for each square foot of substrate area, so that in an aquarium which is 90x45cm (36x18in), 162 plants could be accommodated. From this number you would need to deduct any space taken up by rocks and, of course, that which is allocated as a plant-free swimming zone. This should still enable a lot of plants to be featured. Most aquarists tend to underplant their aquariums in the UK, whereas in continental Europe plants are generally much more of a feature. In the US, underplanting is also more common than the reverse state.

By using planters of various types and stones or bricks to vary their depth below the water, it is possible to grow both emersed and submersed plants in a pond of unvarying depth.

FLOATING PLANTS

These will affect the number of submerged plants because they will deny the latter much light, and opinions differ as to the merits of surface plants. My own view is that they are not worth having in an aquarium, for their trailing roots add nothing to an aquascene, and you will probably not see their leaves anyway because they will be hidden by the canopy. The same is true when they are in ponds; that is, they deny submerged plants

always better off by carrying out routine disinfecting of newly acquired stock—be this in animal or vegetable form. In the case of plants, this is easily done by placing a few crystals of potassium permanganate in water, just enough to turn it a deep pink (not purple). The plants can be placed in this solution for about two hours, which should kill any harmful bacteria they may be carrying. This process should be repeated after any serious outbreak of illness in an aquarium, for the plants could well be shelter to bacteria or to various insects which themselves might be carriers of disease.

sunlight. Additionally most are rampant growers so they virtually become blanket weed, creating the need to continually cull them to contain their spread. They will also restrict your view of the goldfish in a pond, so for one reason or another they have little to recommend them.

DISINFECTING PLANTS

Although plants acquired from reputable sources should be free of problems, the aquarist is

COLDWATER PLANT SPECIES

The newcomer to the aquatic hobby is strongly recommended not to attempt to have a veritable botanical garden in the aquarium but to concentrate on just a few hardy plants in the early stages.

In this way, experience will be gained without the problems associated with attempts to maintain many species in a limited environment. It is much easier to experiment with four species than with eight, for plants do not always mix well together, their requirements often being opposed to those of other species.

The plants included in this text are popular, readily available, and attractive. They are not especially expensive and can be propagated without difficulty. Only basic comments are made on them, so unless stated otherwise it can be assumed that pH, water

Plant plugs provide a rooting medium and also provide fertilizer for live plants. Photo courtesy of Aquarium Products

Facing page: Try to limit the amount of vegetation on the surface of the pond. The more vegetation on top, the less you will see of your fish. Photo: Michael Gilroy

hardness, and temperature requirements are not critical and will be within the range of the average coldwater aquarium. Once experience is gained with hardy plants, then the more delicate or unusual varieties can be selectively tried—first in a nursery tank and then

A large, heavily planted aquarium can serve as home for many different types of nonaggressive fishes, including goldfish if the temperature is not kept too high. Goldfish will readily accept flake foods.

in the main show aquarium. In a goldfish tank which has had a small heater installed in order to control the minimum temperature, then it may be possible to try a few species that are normally considered tropical, for remember that some species of the tropics are found at altitudes where the temperature is often not as warm as might be thought.

POND PLANTS

Most of the plants described in this text will, of course, grow well in ponds, for these and rivers are, of course, their wild habitat. A goldfish pond can feature many flowering plants, of which the most well-known is probably the

A group of veiltails and shubunkins provides grace and beauty in a planted aquarium. Photo: B. Pengilley

success is obviously more likely with species indigenous to your country than with those imported from tropical lands. However, even these may survive during the warmer seasons of temperate climates but will need to be lifted during the fall; otherwise

Top: Acorus gramineus, *dwarf sedge.* **Bottom:** Bacopa caroliniana, *flower.*
Photo: F. Mohlmann

water lily in its many forms. However, many other plants are suited to the pond as either deep water, shallow, marginal, or bog plants. A water garden center is the best place to view these. Pond plants should reflect the climate you live in, because

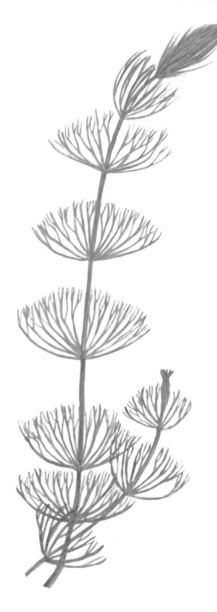

Ceratophyllum submersum, *a hornwort.*

they may be severely damaged by early frosts. Such plants should be pruned of foliage and stored in damp soil in a cool environment until they will be ready for planting in baskets the following spring.

Many wild river plants (such as cattails) will grow too tall for the average garden pond, so where they are required cultivated forms should be acquired. However, I think a garden pond should have only limited plantings if the prime object is to view the goldfish. Plantings should be contained in baskets for convenience.

POPULAR AQUATIC PLANTS
Key to abbreviations:
Dist: Distribution. *Ht:* Height (approx). *Light:* Light intensity. *Prop:* Propagation. *Plant:* Suggested site in aquarium. *Des:* General description and comments.

Acorus gramineus **(Dwarf Sedge; Japanese Rush)**
Dist: E. Asia. *Ht:* 30cm (12 in); also dwarf varieties.

Light: Moderate to bright but very adaptable. *Prop:* Division of rhizome. *Plant:* Fore or middleground. *Des:* Attractive linear leaves of green which may be striped with yellow. Not a true aquatic plant but from marshlands so eventually wilts if immersed for long periods. There are

Left: Elodea canadensis, *one of the most common aquarium plants.* *Above:* Cardamine lyrata *has attractive leaves.*

many cosmopolitan species such as *A. calamus* (Sweet Flag).

Bacopa caroliniana

Dist: N. America: Florida and eastern seaboard. *Ht:* Up to 60cm (24 in) in related forms but generally 30cm (12 in). *Light:*

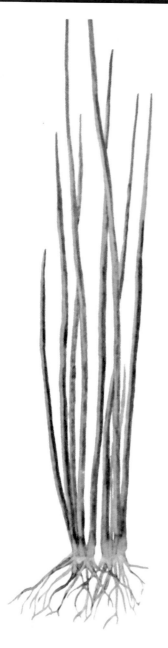

Moderate to bright. *Prop:* Offshoots or cuttings. *Plant:* Middle to background. *Des:* Attractive whorls of small green leaves radiate from tall stem. Plant in bunches of five or seven for best effect. Temperature should not drop below about 15°C (59°F).

Cardamine lyrata (Chinese Ivy; Japanese Cress)

Dist: China, Korea, Japan. The family is distributed globally in the more temperate climates. *Ht:* 38cm (15 in). *Light:* Moderate to bright. *Prop:* Division of rootstock or cuttings. *Plant:* Middle or background in clusters. *Des:* Pale to mid-green round or kidney-shaped leaves on a slender stem. Although delicate looking it is a hardy plant. It is at its best in cooler waters and will wilt if the temperature rises much above 19°-C (66°F).

Ceratophyllum spp. (Hornwort)

Dist: Cosmopolitan. *Ht:* 38cm (15 in). *Light:* Bright. Prop: From cuttings which

Eleocharis acicularis, the familiar hair grass of aquarists.

must be anchored into the substrate as this genus does not have roots on them so will otherwise float. *Plant:* Middle to background. *Des:* Attractive

Above: Hydrilla vetricillata, *one of the plants called elodea by aquarists. Photo: L. Wischnath.* **Left:** *Willow or water moss,* Fontinalis antipyretica.

plant that has whorls of needlelike leaves along the slender stem. In bunches these make a nice display. They are very brittle so handle with care—but they are able to withstand goldfish. They make good

spawning mops when you breed your goldfish. There are several species to choose from: *C. demersum*, *C. submersum*, and *C. echinatum*.

Elodea spp.

Dist: South America. *Ht:* Can attain 4m (13 ft) in rivers. *Light:* Bright. *Prop:* Cuttings or division of root-stock. *Plant:* Background. *Des:* Long-stemmed plants with whorls of linear leaves. An example of tropical plants that prefer cooler waters. A long-time favorite of aquarists. Will live as a free-floating plant as well. Good mixers with many other plants.

Eleocharis acicularis (Hair Grass; Spike Rush)

Dist: Cosmopolitan. *Ht:* 38cm (15 in). *Light:* Moderate to bright. *Prop:* By runners. *Plant:* Fore or middleground. *Des:* Produces tufts of slender grass-like stems which create a carpet effect of outcrops across the substrate.

Top: Ludwigia palustris, *false loosestrife. Photo: Zukal.* **Bottom:** Myriophyllum spicatum, *water milfoil. Photo: L. Wischnath*

A nice contrast to normally leafed plants.

Fontinalis antipyretica (Willow or Water Moss)

Dist: The cooler regions of the Northern Hemisphere. *Ht:* Up to 50cm (20 in). *Light:* Subdued to moderate. *Prop:* By Cuttings. *Plant:* Middleground near rocks which it will cling to. *Des:* A nice deep green, the plant forms bushes of many branched stems which sport tiny leaves. It does not have roots and prefers a position where there is good water movement. Better at the lower temperatures, otherwise it will wilt. A useful spawning plant.

Hydrilla verticillata (Hydrilla)

Dist: Cosmopolitan. *Ht:* 30cm (12 in). *Light:* Moderate to bright. *Prop:* Cuttings. *Plant:* Background. *Des:* Slim-stemmed plant which looks very similar to *Elodea canadensis.* Can be planted or free-floating; it is a hardy, undemanding plant.

Ludwigia palustris (False Loosestrife)

Spatterdock, Nuphar pumilum.

Dist: Cosmopolitan. *Ht:* 38cm (15 in). *Light:* Very bright. *Prop:* Cuttings. *Plant:* Middle or background. *Des:* Long-stemmed plant with green leaves which may become reddish on their underside.

Potamogeton crispus, *pondweed.*

The leaves form opposite pairs and it makes an attractive plant which mixes well with others. Always feature a number of plants for best effect. There are numerous species but the one cited—together with hybrids of it—makes the best aquarium inmate as others often wilt when kept submerged for long periods, for they are basically marsh plants.

Myriophyllum spicatum (Water milfoil)

Dist: Cosmopolitan. *Ht:* 51cm (20 in). *Light:* Bright.

Prop: Cuttings; remove lower leaves. *Plant:* Background. *Des:* A very attractive plant that has a tall thick stem from which radiate whorls of fine feather-like leaves. It is a strong-growing plant but must be provided with clear water free of debris, which will otherwise clog its minute pores. The species cited, together with *M.*

Sagittaria graminea.

verticillatum, is suited to coldwater aquariums—others are better in heated tanks, so select the right species.

Nuphar pumilum (Yellow Lily, Spatterdock)
Dist: Europe. *Ht:* 51cm (20 in). *Light:* Bright. *Prop:* Division of rhizome; be sure it has a growing tip. *Des:* A member of the lily family, this is really a pond plant but can be grown in the larger aquarium where its broad spear-shaped

leaves will add a touch of the tropical to the aquascene. If they outgrow the aquarium, they can be transferred to a pond, though they may not survive the transition. They will be too large for small aquariums.

Potamogeton crispus (Pondweed)

Dist: Cosmopolitan. *Ht:* 38cm (15 in). *Light:* Bright. *Prop:* Division of rhizome or runners. *Plant:* Middle or background. *Des:* Thick stems from which the linear or lanceolate leaves radiate in pairs; the edges of these are curly. Color may range from green to red-brown, so they make a welcome addition to an aquarium. They require a nutrient-rich substrate.

Sagittaria spp.

Dist: Mainly N. America but introduced elsewhere. *Ht:* Very variable according to species. *Light:* Moderate to subdued. *Prop:* By runners. *Plant:* Middleground or background. *Des:* About 38cm (15 in)

in species used in aquariums but can be much larger in pond plants. Leaves long and polymorphic in shape—linear, lanceolate, arrow-shaped and similar. The leaves radiate from substrate level. Numerous species are used in aquaculture, and they are all popular plants exhibiting varying shades of green. Check with your dealer as to which they have and about their requirements—all of which are slightly different.

Vallisneria spiralis

Dist: S. Europe but introduced elsewhere. Ht: 51cm (20 in). *Light:* Bright. *Prop:* By runners. *Plant:* Middle to background. *Des:* Narrow tall green linear leaves that are not unlike the previous species. There is a variety, *tortifolia,* in which the leaves twist in a spiral fashion. One of the oldest of all aquarium plants, it is an undemanding species other than for its requirement for very bright light.

Feeding

The feeding of goldfish is a very easy thing to do because they will consume both plant and animal tissues, such a regimen being called omnivorous. On this basis, if it is a food item and if it will fit into their mouths, then they will eat it with very few exceptions. However, this does not mean that all foods will have the same value to goldfish, so it is important that they be provided with a diet that is both balanced and of good nutritional content.

If a goldfish is fed on poor quality foods, even if this is given in quantity, it will not result in strong healthy growth because it will lack vital ingredients

Hand-feeding goldfish is a pleasant benefit of the hobby. Goldfish are excellent eaters and will take almost anything. Photo: Michael Gilroy

required for body metabolism. In order to appreciate what a balanced diet of quality food comprises, it is important to understand the role of food in the body and which food items can supply that needed to fulfill the role in question.

HOMEMADE FOODS

The cost of feeding a few goldfish is so modest that they must surely be the most inexpensive of all pets as far as their nutritional needs are concerned. In past years, goldfish breeders had to make up their own fish menus because commercial foods were basic and not especially good. Today, however, considerable research goes into the preparation of aquarium foods, and the quality and range are now very impressive indeed. Most owners use prepared foods, but the addition of homemade foods still has a significant role to play in providing variety to the diet.

All such foods should be fresh and, where applicable, carefully washed. The food should be sliced into very small pieces that can be swallowed by the goldfish, though it can be given as larger lumps as well and the fish will enjoy nibbling at it. You can suspend small pieces of meat on a thread, and this will give the fish something to interest them and will prevent the food from falling to the substrate. Remove it after a few hours so it does not start to rot.

Among the homemade foods of value, the following are but a few of the better ones: spinach, carrots, peas, beans, and kale. (Items such as lettuce have very little nutritional value.) Also included are brown bread (toasted or not), crumbled dog biscuits, all lean meats, and any mashes made by mixing these with items such as egg yolk and milk. Of course, sweet sticky foods should not be given to fish.

COMMERCIAL FOODS

Prepared foods may be dried, freeze-dried, or frozen, which means that a considerable range of nutrients is available to aquarists.

Dried Foods

These may be in the form of flakes, pellets, granules, or tablets, each of these giving particular benefits. Flakes are very thin and will float for a while before slowly sinking. They are thus useful for encouraging the fish to the surface. This is especially advantageous where pond goldfish are concerned, as they will thus become much tamer and can be trained to eat special treats from your fingers, such as pieces of meat or cheese. Pellets and granular foods float or sink at varying rates and are useful during the early and late seasons when the goldfish will be at the lower depths; they can still be used in the

Moderate head growth on a calico pom-pon. Extremely large head growths in lionheads, orandas, and similar varieties may make feeding difficult. Photo: Fred Rosenzweig

Flake foods, available in a variety of conveniently sized packages, are among the most commonly offered goldfish foods. Photo courtesy of Wardley

Really poor swimmers, such as this white matt bubble-eye, may have to be handfed. Observe the feeding habits of each of your fish for potential problems. Photo: Fred Rosenzweig.

aquarium as well because the fish will pick at them on the substrate. Tablets can be slow sinkers or they can be stuck onto the glass of the aquarium to form mini-feeding stations.

Frozen Foods

These have brought many natural foods into the menu in a very convenient form. Most popular live foods are now avail-able in frozen form so that they can be stored for long periods for feeding as required. They are hygienic and will float for quite a while and will encourage your goldfish to the surface of the water.

Live foods

These are usually available from your aquatic dealer and, providing they are cultured forms, they will save you the bother of breeding them. The little extra this costs is worth it if you only have a few goldfish. Care should be exercised if collecting live foods from the wild because they may well be carriers of disease or unwanted pests. It is better to obtain live foods from nonfish habitats, or use culture starters available from pet shops; these will sometimes come complete with instructions.

Live Food Types: There is a large range of potential live foods suitable for fish, but in practical terms a small number are especially associated with aquarists. Much liked by the fish and extremely nutritious is *Daphnia*, which is a genus of water fleas. These tiny crustaceans are common in certain natural watercourses and stagnant ponds. They are excellent fry foods and are easily propagated once a starter cul-

ture is obtained from your pet shop. A container of water is left to stand for about 36 hours, and then a small quantity of manure (duck, chicken, or horse) is added to the water. After a few days the water will cloud up with microorganisms on which the *Daphnia* will feed. The culture is then added, and over the following weeks their numbers will build up. They can be drawn off as required, but never take more than about 30% of the *Daphnia* at one time. Otherwise, the vigor of the colony might suffer. The addition of lettuce leaves

Active mid-water feeders such as this ryukin often will chase down live foods. Photo: Dr. Herbert R Axelrod

or bruised apples will be required periodically to ensure that the organisms (infusorians) on which the *Daphnia* feed have themselves got a food supply. The culture water can also be prepared using bruised fruit or vegetables, but manure seems to produce quicker establishment of the microorganisms. The culture must be prepared and maintained with care; otherwise, it will pollute, as it is subject to the same rules of balance as is an aquarium. Periodically it is prudent to start a new culture.

Daphnia can be bred in an outbuilding during the summer but will need a temperature of about 20°C (68°F) minimum during the winter months; otherwise, the culture will cease to multiply. Another similar food is *Cyclops*.

Worms of various sorts are popular aquatic live foods but some, such as *Tubifex* spp., come from rather undesirable habitats, as they are found in badly polluted water or in mud banks at the exit of sewers. They are thin worms up to about 8 cm (3 in) long and red in color. They are greatly enjoyed by the fish but must be well washed for a day or so before being fed to the fish. Place them under a dripping tap if this is possible; otherwise, place them in a shallow plastic tub of water which just covers them. Change the water regularly and you can keep them in your fridge for a week or two. Tubifex can be purchased from your dealer, which is better than your attempting to collect your own; they are also available freeze-dried.

Common earthworms are another live food that can be purchased or collected. Clean them by placing them in a container of sawdust for about 24 hours during which time they will rid themselves of toxins, which will be defecated. Feed them to your goldfish according to the size of your fish.

Swatted (but not sprayed) flies will provide

variety to the goldfish menu as will other land insects. Many can now be purchased from commercial companies who specialize in a whole range of creepy-crawlies that are supplied for aquarists and reptile keepers. It should be mentioned that cyprinids show no parental feelings for their own offspring, so that these are also another live food source to them. Attempts to breed in an aquarium where the parents are retained with the fry will result in many of the latter being eaten.

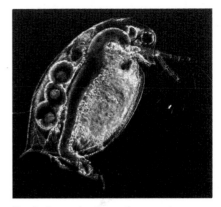

Daphnia *and other microcrustaceans are an excellent food for goldfish and are easily purchased, collected, or raised. Photo: Engasser*

AMOUNTS TO FEED

The quantity of food eaten will reflect the temperature and other environmental conditions.

These factors not withstanding, the amount of food given to the goldfish at any one time should be that which is consumed in about 5-10 minutes. It is desirable to feed a little and often, as this is how the fish would eat in the wild. There is another consideration regarding food quantity and this relates to the quality of the food. Dried foods will contain a very high ratio of nutrient to water, whereas live foods contain about 70% water. The fish will thus be satiated more readily with small quantities of highly nutritious food than if given poor quality food. Live food is not poor quality, of course, but on a weight-for-weight basis the fish will need more of this in order to extract a weight of protein comparable to that found in a high-protein flake food. Likewise, plant-based dried foods will have concentrated nutrients whereas fresh plants will be mainly water in content so will be required in more bulk, comparatively speaking. Do remember that dried foods have a very definite shelf life, and this may be stated on the packaging. Special offers of one package free if buying a given number of packages are worthwhile only if you can use them up within their shelf life.

It is best to feed your goldfish at a regular time each day because in this way you will not only find the fish eager and waiting for their meal, but you will more easily spot any showing no interest. This is less likely if they are fed at varying times against no particular schedule. Do not, however, feed late in the evening, as the extra oxygen needed for digestion will be used at a time when this is at it lowest level in the aquarium, unless it is well aerated or comfortably understocked.

Another recommendation regarding the feeding routine, if your goldfish are a hobby for your entire family, is to establish who will be responsible for feeding the fish. This should be done on a regular rotation basis or by just one person. It is very easy to overfeed (and pollute the tank) if every person who comes in says, "I wonder if the fish have been fed?" and promptly gives them a helping to add to that which everyone else has given them! The problems that will arise from such a mismanaged situation are obvious.

Always make a point of watching the fish eat because, as in most animal species, there are the greedy and the timid eaters. In such cases, the latter can be fed at one end of the tank while the gluttons are being fed at the other end. One of the disadvantages of ring feeders for worms, and similar feeding utensils, is that the more aggressive fish take the lion's share—-probably more than is good for them.

VACATION TIME

When it is time for your annual vacation, it is not important that the fish are fed while you are away—provided, of course, they are in excellent health. Well-intentioned friends or neighbors will do more harm than good if left to feed your fish, because they will invariably overdo this. You may return to find a badly polluted tank. Goldfish will survive for up to three weeks without a problem, because there is always natural food in a planted aquarium.

Alternatively, leave only a very small quantity of food along with instructions that the fish are on a special health dict, and it is vital this is not exceeded while you are away.

IROAGE

This term is Japanese and it means bringing out the best color of a fish. It is extensively used with koi but is equally applicable to any species. In its narrowest meaning it is applied to the feeding of special foods which are rich in nutrients that aid color-forming pigments. In its correct use, it applies to the whole aquatic environment in which the fish live. Any color foods suited to koi are fine for goldfish, but do remember that excess use of these will actually ruin the colors and make white look pinkish and red look brassy. You can highlight color in fish, but you cannot put it where it is not already featured. If you feed a well planned diet that already includes items containing carotene, color feeding will add little to your fish, so if they are poorly colored then the probable answer is to purchase better fish.

Fresh, clean tubifex worms are accepted by most goldfish and are readily purchased. Photo: W. Tomey

Breeding

Goldfish are very straightforward in their breeding requirements, unlike many tropical fish, which can be very difficult. However, any person contemplating breeding any sort of animal should have a very sound reason for so doing. To breed simply for its own sake, that is, to reproduce the species, has little merit in aquatic circles. There should be a more ambitious objective in mind and this will normally be to create a pool of better quality fish, to improve the color, or to try to create a new variety by crossings involving established varieties or even differing species. Each of these is a highly specialized undertaking, and the latter two objectives are better delayed until one has gained breeding experience and a very full knowledge of the goldfish.

It must be remembered that goldfish are farmed on a commercial scale in many countries, so there is no shortage of average-type fish—evidenced by the very inexpensive prices that the very popular varieties command. From this it can be said that those who think they can make some quick money breeding goldfish will be in for a very disappointing time. The already low price at which you can purchase fish is not what you can obtain as a breeder; the dealer's margin must be deducted from that and this leaves very little for small operators. Goldfish, like koi, are big business, and commercial farms can produce them far cheaper than can the average hobbyist.

However, there is good news as well. Commercial farms are far less able to produce quality goldfish,

As with many other coldwater fish, the sexes of goldfish can be difficult to determine until breeding begins. Even then, the fish are better able to determine their sex than is the aquarist. Photos: J. Elias

because these require much more individual attention.

There is always a market for such fish, and the fact they are "homebred," that is, well acclimatized to the conditions of your country, and from known parentage, is a definite plus.

BREEDING STOCK

It is important that you commence any breeding program with the finest examples possible. Do not breed fish that were purchased as inexpensive pets. It takes just as long, and just as much food, to feed inferior stock as it does that which is of merit. It is also better to commence with the varieties that are hardy and not unduly modified in their anatomy: the common goldfish, the comet or maybe the shubunkin. Visit a number of goldfish exhibitions so you can see what good stock looks like. You will also be able to discuss your interests with breeders of your favored variety. They will have stock available

for sale in many cases. Do not crossbreed varieties until you have gained good experience. Although one male may be paired with a female, it is usually found that two are better, but they should be well matched for their quality.

SEXING

Goldfish are sexually dimorphic only when in breeding condition. At this time the male will develop white pin-head-sized spots on his gill covers and the immediate area around these; such dots are known as tubercles. The female will appear more rounded as she fills up with developing eggs; when viewed from above her shape will be more rounded on one side than the other.

BREEDING AGE

Females should not be used for breeding until they

Facing page: Breeding in goldfish involves a great deal of chasing and splashing, with eggs and sperm everywhere. For the aquarist, this strongly limits the type of aquarium in which goldfish can successfully reproduce. Photos: J. Elias

are two years old (they will then be fully mature). They will breed before this age but their offspring will probably be less vigorous. Males can be used from one year of age providing they are strong, healthy examples. There is not really an upper breeding age, but quality of the young will start to diminish once the females reach about 5-6 years of age.

METHOD OF REPRODUCTION

Goldfish, like the majority of the world's animals, are egglayers, and this form of reproduction is known as oviparity, as compared with ovoviviparity, which is when the young develop within the female's body to an advanced stage before she releases young, or viviparity, when the young are

To be successful, the spawning aquarium should be heavily planted. Photo: J. Elias

born in an advanced state—as in most mammals (the monotremes being egglayers). Goldfish are egg scatterers which, as the name suggests, lay their eggs in a random manner, though they do try to select a suitable spawning medium to which the eggs will adhere. When a species adopts this method of reproduction, the survival strategy is based on the premise that if you produce enough offspring, a few will survive to perpetuate the species, so goldfish will lay a few thousand eggs during spawning activities. In the wild, the vast majority of these would perish, for predators would take them (including their parents and other fish), or they would be infected by a disease or they would be infertile. Under domesticated conditions, it is possible for most to be reared, but this is not a practical reality if one is attempting to producc good goldfish, so

The male is more easily recognized by his chasing of the female than by any readily visible external characters. Photo: J. Elias

it is normal practice for the breeder to act as nature would and cull the majority, maybe retaining as few as 10%, by the end of the culling program.

BREEDING METHODS

There are two ways in which goldfish can be bred: by uncontrolled or controlled programs. In the former, there is no attempt to be selective about which fish breed with which, whereas in the latter the owner selects the fish which are required as parental stock. In this way "type" (as well as color) can be improved. Left on their own, the goldfish will produce a very heterogeneous collection of offspring. This is because the eggs of a single female may be fertilized by the sperm of many males. Of course, only one male can fertilize any single egg, it being a case that if five males are in breeding condition, the offspring will have a single mother but could have one of five fathers, so the range of potential bodily forms

and colors could be considerable. Those who have no breeding facilities, such as the average pond owner, will probably use this method but they will not produce any good goldfish. Apart from any other consideration, it must be remembered that in uncontrolled breeding one cannot assume the best fish will survive—only the toughest will, and invariably they are the least pleasing to look at! Controlled breeding is therefore the only option for serious hobbyists, be they aquarium or pond owners.

BREEDING CONDITION

This term simply means that the breeding stock are fit and ready to breed. During the spring the prospective breeding fish should be given a diet rich in proteins. Live foods are especially beneficial at this time. Some weeks before spawning is expected, it can be beneficial to separate the sexes, as this usually results in greater eagerness to reproduce once

This egg-laden female shows the expanded abdomen typical of spawning females. Photo: J. Elias

the sexes are reintroduced to each other. It is not essential, though it again gives the owner a little bit more control in determining, to some degree, when the actual spawning will take place.

FERTILIZATION

The sexual act in goldfish does not involve any sort of union between the sexes. After a period of courtship, in which the males chase the female around the spawning tank in order to encourage her to shed her eggs, she will eventually do so. The attendant males will then shed their sperm onto the eggs in a whitish cloud referred to as milt. Many sperm will fail to make contact with an egg, but a number will do so and thus the egg will be fertilized and embryonic development of the fry will commence. Hundreds of eggs may be left unfertilized and will simply shrivel up or be eaten by the numerous microorganisms within the water. Even fertilized eggs may not develop to full term, for a bacterium might gain access to the egg and kill it. Others may have genetic faults that prevent normal development and so only a percentage of all eggs shed will develop to the fry stage. At the point of fertilization it is therefore important that the water condition be excellent.

BREEDING TEMPERATURE

The water temperature at which fish breed is very important in temperate climate species, for it must coincide with a period when there will be an abundance of plant and animal life for the fry to feed on. Breeding cycles of many species of water inhabitants are thus closely interrelated to each other. The spring and the summer are the times when goldfish breed; the temperature required is in the order of 18-20°C (64-68°F). Fish that have been kept over winter at a reduced temperature are more likely to breed with greater vigor than those kept at a constant temperature. In the former case, natural cycles are taking place, so the fish reach breeding condition as the temperature increases.

BREEDING TANKS

Shortly before the fish are due to spawn, breeding tanks should be prepared. Their size is not critical, but a typical one would be about 60 x 38 x 30 cm. (L x W x D), which is 24 x 15 x 12 in. Length

Goldfish are not averse to eating their own eggs. Eggs that are not hidden in the plants may not survive. Photo: J. Elias

is the most important consideration, as this gives the fish plenty of room to go about the courting ritual. With cyprinids this is a pretty hectic affair involving much chasing and bumping, whereby fins can be torn and scales lost.

The tank should contain water to a depth of about 23 cm (9 in) or a little more. A sponge filter will help clean the water and provide gentle aeration. The water should be added a day or so before the fish so that its chlorine content is virtually nil and it has a settled oxygen level. The best site for a breeding tank is where it will receive at least some early morning sun rays, as these stimu-

Unless there are many plants or spawning mops in the aquarium, the odds are good that the parents will eat most of their eggs. In pond situations this is less likely because of the very size of the bottom when compared to even a large aquarium.
Photo: J. Elias

late the female to shed her eggs. The actual spawning will normally take place during the morning and will terminate about mid-day.

SPAWNING MEDIUM

Opinions vary on what is the best spawning medium, so here we will consider the options. The most obvious option is no medium at all. That is, the eggs simply fall to the bare aquarium floor. The problem is that rather a lot will be eaten. You can improve matters by placing a fine plastic mesh just above the base so the eggs fall through but the adults cannot reach them.

Another option is to place glass marbles on the floor; these are inert and the eggs will fall between them so most will be safe from the parents. More popular is the use of plastic or real plants onto which the eggs will adhere; the plants should be placed in small tubs. The most popular method of all these days is to use commercial spawning mops, available from your aquatic dealer. These are inert and will catch the

falling eggs. Even small branches from fir trees can be used as mops, for their prime purpose is simply to provide a safe haven for the eggs.

HATCHING THE EGGS

Once the spawning has taken place the parents should be removed and returned to their communal or separate tanks, the latter being preferable since it will stop the female from being chased any longer (which might otherwise be the case if they remain together). Once the parents have been removed you can reduce the water level to about 15 cm (6 in). This is so that as the fry hatch they can easily reach the water surface, where they will inflate their swim-bladders and become free-swimming independent goldfish. The time taken for the eggs to hatch is determined by the temperature. If this is about 20°C (68°F), then the process will be completed in 4-5 days. At lower temperatures it will take a tittle longer, while at higher figures it will be slightly quicker (but this is not advised, for excess heat may adversely affect the eggs).

Unhatched eggs may develop a fungus on them, but if the water is clean this is unlikely to affect the fertilized eggs. Water disinfectants are available from your supplier. The product chosen must be specially designed for this use; otherwise it can kill the unhatched embryos. You could, of course, attempt to remove unfertilized eggs (which will remain a gray-white color) but this is a tedious chore.

REARING THE FRY

During the first 48 hours after hatching, the fry will gain their nutrient needs from the remains of their yolk sacs, but once they have become free-swimming they will need a very regular supply of food. This must be prepared in advance so it is ready the minute they are swimming. There are three popular fry foods available: infusorians, which are tiny ciliates, brine shrimp nauplii, which are the young of *Artemia salina*, and commercial fry foods, which may be liquid or powder.

Infusoria cultures can be prepared by adding bruised banana skins, hay, or bruised vegetables to cooled boiled water placed into a glass jar. The water

Many breeders treat the eggs with methylene blue to reduce the incidence of fungal and bacterial infections before hatching. Photo: Dr. Herbert R. Axelrod

will initially turn cloudy and smell but will then clear as the culture develops. Only when it has lost its pungent smell is it ready to be given to the fry. It can then be poured into the fry tank or, better, drip fed. To do this place a length of plastic piping from the jar to the tank. The jar must be placed higher than the tank surface for the siphon to operate. An air-line clip can be used to regulate the supply. You will need a number of jars being prepared so that there is a ready supply until the fry are large enough to accept other foods; this will be after about 7-14 days. I should state that while infusoria is an inexpensive means of providing suitable live food for fry, which is important, they are not especially nutritious, so it is better if you can offer the fry more substantial foods at the earliest opportunity.

Brine shrimp is now the most widely used fry food. The eggs can be purchased from your dealer, and they

No fancy goldfish breeding produces only young that resemble the parent variety; no variety breeds true 100% of the time. For this reason, constant culling of deficient fry is necessary. Photo: J. Elias

can be stored convenient-
ly. Cultures are made ei-
ther by purchasing a
hatchery unit from an
aquatic dealer or by using
glass jars. Cool water is
placed into the jar and to
this is added marine salt
(but cooking salt can also
be used) in the strength of
3% (30g per liter). The jar(s)
should be kept in a warm
room with a tempera-
ture of about 22°C
(72°F) and it
must be well
aerated. The
shrimp eggs
are added at
the required
rate, which will
depend on the
number of fish and
the size of the culture
jar. Hatching takes 24-
48 hours, after which the
newly hatched nauplii are
gathered by siphoning the
culture water into a fine
net, which is then swirled
in the rearing tank. The
strained water can be
poured back into the cul-
ture jar. If you use a large
jar, it is beneficial to include a small air diffuser

stone, as shrimp prefer
good oxygenation. Once
they hatch, you can sepa-
rate the shrimp from their
shells and unhatched eggs
simply by turning off the
air supply for a few min-
utes. The shrimp will swim
an inch or two from the
bottom of the jar and can be
siphoned off to be placed
through a net as al-
ready described.

*Basic breeds: A typical oranda.
Notice the dorsal fin and head
growths*

Brine shrimp will live only
a short while in fresh water, so feed small amounts
but as often as possible.
Commercial fry foods
should be given as direct-
ed on their labels. It is
most important that fry be

very well supplied with food, as they grow at a rapid rate. However, care must be exercised in order that too much is not given, which will pollute the water. In the first weeks of the fry's lives, the tank illumination should remain on for 24 hours a day. This will encourage rapid growth.

The fry, like their parents, are cannibalistic, so the bigger ones will eat any weak or deformed ones

Basic breeds: A red crucian carp, a wild cousin of the fancy goldfish.

that will fit into their mouths. This is not something you should worry over, because it is a natural process—though after the first few days it is not desirable because some of the better fish may be consumed.

It is important that partial water changes are made in the rearing tank every week (or even every 4-5 days) in order to reduce the risk of bacterial buildup; the tank must also be gently but well filtered and aerated. If external filters are used, keep your eyes on them, as some fry might just find their way into the filter chambers. If at all possible the fry should be divided so that they are placed in two or more rearing tanks, which will reduce the risk of disease and lower the cannibalistic rate which might result from overcrowding. The water level in the rearing tank, reduced initially, can be filled to its normal level once all of the fry are free-swimming.

HAND STRIPPING
There are a few reasons why it is desirable to hand-strip a pair of goldfish. An

obvious one is that the fish in question have a known low fertility rate and hand stripping will certainly improve this. Such fish would have to be something special, because it is never good breeding practice to use fish that have poor fertility rates.

A more likely reason is simply to obtain maximum fertilization of the eggs. Some of the more fancy varieties seem to have great-

vigor until the artificial means becomes not just the "norm" but virtually obligatory. Experimental breeders often hand strip in order to ensure fertilization when crossing differing, but related, species. Finally, it may simply be a case of convenience in that your fish are clearly about to spawn but you must go away during the day. Unless the fish are hand

Basic breeds: A ryukin of the ribbontail variety.

stripped, on your return you could find that many eggs have been devoured.

er difficulty in spawning, so a helping hand may be desirable. However, when a variety cannot reproduce naturally, I would seriously question its worth. From studies in other animal groups it is clear that regular use of "artificial" means of propagating species tends to reduce their

The method is quite simple. Prepare three small bowls with water taken from the breeding tank, and place each of the parents into a separate bowl. In the third, place a small spawning mop or some color-fast cloth (duly weighted down). Carefully take hold of the male and place him in the third bowl (holding him under water, of course). Gently use your index finger and thumb to squeeze out his sperm by moving from his mid-body line toward his vent. You will see a stringy white thread emerge and this will break up as it enters the water. Place him back into his bowl and gently stir the water to distribute the sperm.

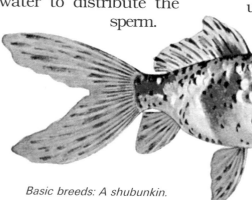

Basic breeds: A shubunkin.

Repeat this process with the female, but move her around so the eggs are scattered over the area of the cloth or other spawning medium. Place her back and then again gently stir the water. Leave this bowl as it is for about 15 minutes in order for the sperm to penetrate the eggs and com-

mence fertilization. After this time they can be transferred to the hatching tank.

You can strip the parents twice or maybe even three times in this manner, after which they can be returned to their usual tank. Do not attempt to strip out all the eggs or all the sperm as you could, in so doing, damage the fish. Likewise, never attempt to hand-strip fish unless you are certain both are in full breeding condition for, again, this could result in injury to the parents. The beginner is advised to have an experienced aquarist on hand on the first occasion to ensure the procedure is done correctly. The care of the eggs after being stripped then carries on as already detailed.

CULLING
The process of selecting which fish will and will not live is called culling. It is a

necessary process that no breeder enjoys doing but is a hard reality of life. The extent of culling is very much a personal matter. There are those who remove only obviously deformed fish and those who, by timed selection stages, reduce the number of fish to a very small percent of the original spawning. During the first few selections, the discarded fish are invariably destroyed, but subsequent culling may merely mean that the fish will be sold as pets because they do not show the quality the breeder is looking for. To cull fish that are deformed or will clearly have no market whatsoever can be justified on the grounds that not to do so could mean they will die in pain later or will be disposed of once they become adults, because no one really wants them. The breeding of any

animal species always involves those hard-to-make and often sad decisions, and the potential breeder is wiser to consider these aspects before embarking on a breeding program of any sort.

Selection of the fry is best done initially with the help of a good hand lens. While some breeders select on a weekly or month-

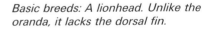

Basic breeds: A lionhead. Unlike the oranda, it lacks the dorsal fin.

ly basis, others do this as a day-to-day continual process. Initially, you will be looking for any deformed fish and any with no pigmentation at all—albinos—for these will have no value whatsoever. Any that seem unusually small compared to the average of the spawning are invariably termed "runts" and retaining them is unlikely to be worthwhile; finally, any that clearly have difficulty swimming or balancing correctly in the water are again of no value, as they may well get worse as they get older.

By the time the fry are about eight weeks

Basic breeds: A common goldfish with no obvious finnage or body modifications.

old they may be reaching a length of about 3.8 cm (1.5 in). Before this stage is reached the number per tank should have been reduced.

The smaller the number that can be placed in a stock rearing tank the better, because only by having maximum space will the young fry attain maximum growth. Never attempt to breed more fish than can be accommodated in a satisfactory manner as they start to grow. Once the initial one or two cullings have been made, then the remaining goldfish will be retained on a best-only basis, for there is no point in feeding inferior fish if you wish to build up a line of potential show-quality exhibits. The total time needed to complete your selection process may be as long as two years; over this period good-looking youngsters can fail to achieve hoped-for potential while other goldfish, not overly impressive when young, may steadily improve with each passing year. Good selection can only come from observation of utterly thousands of fish. It must be remembered that as the fish grow, you should not be comparing them directly against adults but against what quality fish look like when they are immature. For example, a youngster with a real impressive veiltail may catch your eye, but it will likely disappoint you as it matures, for by this time the tail will be too big. A quite attractive, if slightly lightcolored, fish will be less attractive as the years go by because the intensity of color will dilute; a very strongcolored fish with intense pigmentation will develop into a most attractive adult because the intensity will be just about right by the time it is mature. A large head in a youngster usually indicates it will make a good size when mature. The size of the caudal peduncle is also a useful guide to eventual size.

Any potential breeders are strongly advised to join their national goldfish society and their local one. Much help and information will be available from experienced members, and the newsletters will contain very helpful hints on all aspects of keeping these fish.

HEREDITY

All livestock breeders should have a basic understanding of the way in which features are passed from one

Basic breeds: A moor. All moors are black, so the term "black moor" is somewhat redundant.

generation to the next—heredity—for it is a useful aid in any breeder's "tool kit" of knowledge. It will not enable you to be sure of producing better goldfish but will simply explain why given results work out as they do. Knowing this, one is then better able to plan certain crossings involving one's fish. Applied with thought, and in conjunction with judicious selection, which is the cornerstone of any worthwhile program, the chance of improving one's stock rises considerably.

Unfortunately, however, the present knowledge of the transmission of color and bodily features is not especially good in goldfish or koi (or fish generally, for that matter). One thing you will not find in most goldfish books is any reference to genetics in any thorough-going way. Here, very basic principles are detailed which, it is hoped, may provide a platform for further study. In this respect, TFH publishes a useful book titled *Goldfish Breeding and Genetics*, by Joseph Smartt and James H. Bundell, which is highly recommeded.

The practical application of genetics in respect to colors of fish is very complex, which no doubt accounts for the present lack of information on them, but this situation will change in the coming years because greater study is now being undertaken to

A common goldfish going through its color change. Goldfish generally become more colorful as they grow older. Photo: Andre Roth

A rare callco lionhead. Photo: Fred Rosenzweig

sort out the genotypes of both goldfish and koi.

GENES

The features of an animal are determined by small units of coded information within all body cells. These are called genes, and for every feature there is always a pair of genes (there are normally, however, very many pairs, as most features are polygenic). Each parent contributes one gene of each pair so no one parent can pass on both genes of a pair. It is for this reason that those who advise that the female (or the male) is the most important are in error. The reasons why one sex may have greater importance are not related to the transmission of features but to more practical aspects. For example, a quality female can have her eggs fertilized by many males at a single spawning, so all the offspring will carry genes that are 50% from her and the balance from the males. Her genes can thus be perpetuated rapidly within the population of your stock; the reverse can be achieved by hand-stripping a male so that his sperm covers the eggs of two or three females.

All breeding programs involving domesticated species are based on the theory of restricting the gene population so that genes for good quality are retained, while those for poor quality are removed (by selection). On this basis, the overall quality of the fish at each generation gets better—in theory, that is!

Such success presupposes the selection process was good and that desired features are in no way linked to less desirable features. It must also be appreciated that a fish's genes give it a potential for a given quality. Whether or not that potential is achieved is another matter that is determined by environmental conditions. The best goldfish in the world can be ruined in the wrong conditions; conversely, a very moderate fish, in genetic terms, can appear far better than its genotype might suggest if reared by an expert fishkeeper who provided ideal conditions. These very variable permutations make breeding difficult because a good-looking fish may well not produce offspring of the same status, which can frustrate the novice. Again, a knowledge of genetics will explain why this is so and thus lessen the frustration.

PURITY OF GENES

The ways in which gene pairs come together will not only affect the look of a goldfish but will also control how that fish breeds. Distinction should therefore be made between the external appearance of a fish (its phenotype) and the gene pairs that produced such an appearance—the genotype. In understanding this aspect it is necessary to appreciate certain other features of gene action. Genes never mix to create a halfway stage of a feature but always retain their own identity. If an apparent blending is observed, it is the result of other reasons. Let us take a look at a very simple example of gene action in goldfish which will explain one or two important points.

If a wild-type goldfish is paired to an albino goldfish, then all of the offspring will have wild-type coloration. We can show this by using letters to represent genes, so in this case the wild type color has the letters *CC* while the albino has *cc*. Two letters are used for the wild type because the goldfish inherited a gene for this from each parent. When such genes are for the same gene expression they are termed homozygous—they are purebreeding; if they are for a differing expression, then they are heterozygous, non-pure-breeding. In our example, both parents are thus homozygous for their genes.

The reason the letter *C* is chosen to represent the wild type color is because this stands for full color expression. The *cc* is used for albino because this is the alternative form of the gene. In this instance it represents the opposite state—non-full-color or,

	C	C
C	Cc	Cc
C	Cc	Cc

Homozygous pairing

put another way, no color. The same letter must be used when considering alternatives of the same gene, otherwise we would soon get really mixed up when much larger formulas are being calculated. The capital is used for the wild type because it is what is known as a dominant gene, as compared to albino, which is created by a recessive gene. When a dominant gene pairs with a recessive gene, it has the effect of masking it. The

	C	c
C	CC	Cc
c	Cc	cc

Heterozygous pairing

recessive gene is still there, but you just do not see it. Imagine placing a black brick in front of a white brick in a two-brick wall. The white bricks do not show unless you remove the first wall.

Now, during the process of forming gametes, female eggs and male sperm, the paired genes are separated so that only one gene is carried by the egg or the sperm. When these unite to form a zygote (the embryo), the pair of genes are thus restored to the new animal so created. It is pure chance which gene is passed on of a given pair.

In our example it will not affect the end result, because each parent has only one gene type to pass—either a *C* or a *c*. This means that every single offspring must inherit a C from one parent and a *c* from the other. It thus has a genotype of *Cc*, and because *C* is dominant to *c* it will have wild type color. It does not matter which parent is the wild type because, in this instance, the color is not in any way related to the sex of the goldfish. The first generation are thus all heterozygous, non-purebreeding for their color. They can be referred to as full color split for albino and this would be written thus: full color/albino. That before the oblique line is visual, that behind it is carried but hidden. The terms used here are not specific to goldfish, or fish, but are applied to all animal life, because the theory of genetics applies to all life.

PAIRING HETEROZYGOTES

If the male and female offspring of our original mating are paired to each other, then we can prove the genes remained as individual units of heredity. Cc x Cc gives more potential permutations because here each parent can pass on either a C or a c, and these may unite at random with either of the opposite partner's C or c. The full permutations will thus be CC, Cc, cC, and cc (Cc and cC are exactly the same in appearance). Of all of the offspring produced, 75% would be normal wild color and 25% would be albino. Of the 75% wild type, a third would be purebreeding while two-thirds would be heterozygous just as their parents were. Put another way, 25% of all offspring would be homozygous wild type, 50%, would be heterozygous wild type, and 25% would be homozygous albino. There is no visual difference between the purebreeding wild types CC and the non-pure Cc types, and only a series of test matings can establish which are which. Thus it can be seen how two apparently similar fish can have differing breeding potential. If you wanted to establish a pure strain of wild types, then you must purchase known CC stock otherwise you will, sooner or later, find albinos turning up, and it will be a very costly operation to establish which of your fish do not carry the albino gene. Recessive genes are extremely difficult to remove if they are for undesirable features, but very useful if for desired traits. This is because any fish exhibiting a known recessive gene is, of course, homozygous for it. Those with dominant features, genetically speaking, may or may not be pure for them, so may not pass them on to all of their offspring.

It must be stated that in all genetic calculations expectations are based on large numbers; over smaller numbers the percentages may not work out exactly. This is because of the random way genes may unite.

SCALATION

Using this same basic principle of heredity, we can predetermine the type of scalation of our goldfish. The normal metallic scales we can represent by the letter M and those which have no reflective layer by m. If two goldfish which are MM are paired, then only MM offspring can be produced. Likewise, if two mm fish are paired, all of the fry will be non-reflective, or matt, in appearance. When MM and mm are paired, the genotype of the offspring will be Mm which, based on our previous knowledge, should produce all metallic fry of Mm genotype. However-

er, it does not, but instead produces 100% fry with nacreous scales. Here we have apparent blending of genes, but the actual reason is because of what is known as incomplete dominance. The metallic genes have not exerted their full expression, and the result is that the reflective layer thickness is reduced to produce the characteristic mother-of-pearl sheen. In some areas of the fish, the expression may be total—thus the appearance of full metallic shine to the scales. Likewise, the opposite may happen, and there could be patches which show no sheen at all, so they are matt.

In such cases we thus have a third phenotype resulting from just two contrasting gene pairs. This being so, we can then consider what will happen if a nacreous Mn is paired to a metallic MM. The result will be MM, MM, nM, and nM, which is 50% metallic and 50% nacreous. You can easily calculate the other combinations, which we

Two Sarassa (red and white) orandas with nice deep bodies. Photo: Burkhard Kahl

can summarize as follows:

Nacreous x Nacreous = 25% Metallic, 50% Nacreous, 25% Matt

Nacreous x Matt = 50% Nacreous, 50% Matt.

SEX DETERMINATION

The ratio of males to females in any spawning is theoretically 50:50, and is easily shown using our basic knowledge. The male has two dissimilar sex chromosomes, one being known as the X, while the other, much shorter, is known as the Y; the female has two Xs. Goldfish are thus like mammals in this respect, but other fish may reverse the situations, as do birds, so that the female is XY. Any permutation of XY and XX will produce XX and XY, thus equal numbers of each sex. However, in reality there may well be a greater number of one sex than the other due to the random nature of gene action. There may also be other natural processes of selection that, from time to time, favor the development of one or the other of the sexes.

CHROMOSOMES AND LOCI

Genes are always arranged in an orderly manner and are kept together by cytoplasm. The full arrangement of a set of genes is known as a chromosome. It is invariably likened to a string of beads in which the genes are the beads and the string is that which holds them together. They are found in all body cells in pairs, and each chromosome of a pair therefore has its own array of genes. At any given point on the chromosome, the gene on the opposite chromosome of the pair will be for the same feature though, as we have seen, the expression of that gene may be variable depending on whether or not the gene has mutated at any point. The actual spot where a gene is sited is known as

A trio of bright orange orandas with large head growths. Photo: Dr. Herbert R. Axelrod

A nice quality blue-scale oranda with a nice balance of head growth versus body and fins. It is fully hooded, with no brown patches as so often seen on bluescales. Photo: Burkhard Kahl

its locus (plural, loci). It is important to appreciate that at any locus there can be only one allele (alternative) to that on the other chromosome; in other words, regardless of how many times a gene mutates, a goldfish can only carry two examples, at most, of the gene mutations known to exist at that loci. However, if the mutations are at other loci, then any number can be carried by the one fish—thus scale type, color, fin type, head, and eye types are all at differing loci, so can be exhibited by the one goldfish, which is why there are so many varieties to choose from. Colors are controlled by numerous loci, so a goldfish may exhibit an interesting range of these; their intensity and pattern may be polygenically controlled or may be determined by gene modifiers which intensify or dilute it, depending on other genes at other loci which exert influence over it. As color breeders unravel the jigsaw of pieces that make up coloration in goldfish, this area will create a growing need to use genetics in order to successfully predetermine how these may be recombined to good effect by the average breeder.

POLYGENIC ACTION

While we can explain many things by simple example using a single pair of genes—as with albinism—it should be understood that no feature is actually determined by a single pair of such genes. Generally, many genes are involved, which is easily seen by looking at any variety of

A calico oranda. The white areas should be more blue to make a better specimen. Photo: Burkhard Kahl

Calico orandas. The reddish areas could be expected to increase in size and density with growth. Photo: Burkhard Kahl

goldfish. Let us consider size, for example. The potential range of this aspect is vast because, taken in increments of one millimeter, you could have fish ranging from a few inches to nearly a foot. To make this possible, it is very probable that the feature is determined on a buildup basis rather than by individual major gene action, as in basic color. Such features are thus called polygenic features.

As it happens, size in goldfish is also controlled by the environment. This merely complicates matters, unless the breeder ensures there is ample space for the goldfish's growth.

PRACTICAL BREEDING

A basic knowledge of genetics can be very helpful to the goldfish breeder simply because a number of informative conclusions can be drawn. First, it is essential that one knows the genotype of one's breeding stock as far as is possible. This can only be reasonably assessed by seeing other stock from the same parents or strain, which will establish the degree of homozygosity for given features, and the overall quality of features that are polygenically controlled, such as type. It is not sufficient simply to purchase from a breeder at a show, because his or her one winner may not be typical of the breeding average—which just could be pretty bad! See the home stock, if possible, and this will tell you a lot about the likely general genotype. The more variable the stock, the more variable will be the breeding expectations from it. Thus, you need to commence with fish that are likely to produce a very consistent standard.

Once your basic breeding stock has been selected, do not introduce other fish without very considerable thought, otherwise all your efforts could be undone in a single generation. You should not add a fish to your breeding nucleus just because it is an outstanding fish. Many a "star" animal has proved to be a total waste of time in a breeding program simply because it was one of a random combination of genes that just came "right" in that one fish—rather like a winning ticket in a lottery. This said, the fish clearly has the genes for quality; if it comes at the right price, then maybe you could commence a separate line with it rather than using it in your established lines which are producing high quality stock consistently. Extra fish of a strain should be acquired for a definite purpose: to improve a weak point in your own breeding. Such fish will not be

A Chinese ryukin with excellent finnage and deep markings. Because goldfish genetics is so complicated, it is essential that you breed together only the very best specimens of any variety. Photo: Fred Rosenzweig

overexaggerated for the desired feature, because this will merely increase the genetic variability of your gene population. They should be excellent examples of the feature yet show no particular weakness (even if no great merit) in their other features. A big checkbook is not the answer to quality breeding; a good eye for a sound fish is.

The successful breeders are always hoping for a really outstanding fish, but basically their philosophy is that this is more likely to be achieved from consistency rather than from random matings on a best-to-best basis—which leaves the breeder with some good fish but also with a lot of rubbish! As a result, line breeding is the most popular form of breeding. In this method you simply base your policy on the virtues of one or two excellent fish. The object is to retain all of their best features while removing, by selection, any faults that appear in their offspring. By keeping the program restricted to relatives of the chosen goldfish, the population you have will, hopefully, become progressively more pure for the original features selected.

By definition, linebreeding must involve inbreeding, of which it is a dilute form. Close inbreeding will fix in qualities—and faults—very rapidly. The obvious advantage is that you can see what virtues and faults you have in your stock and then proceed to try to eliminate the faults. Close inbreeding, however, carries the risk that if a condition is being carried in a heterozygous state, it increases the chance of producing the homozygous genotype. This is the one which may be lethal, or harmful, in certain arrangements. I know of no lethal genes, at this time, in goldfish, but even so, inbreeding to a high degree (such as father-daughter level) should not be practiced until considerable breeding experience has been gained.

It is essential that breeding records are kept because our memory is rarely accurate on details over any time span. Records should include the fertility rate and the overall health record of fish; unless one retains both in a strain, it is not progressing at all, even if quality is improving. Selection is of vital importance: you must compare like with like all of the time. For example, if you are seeking to improve finnage above all these, then any fish which may attract your eye because of some other feature should not suddenly be upgraded in your mind. Once you have decided on priorities, stick with them until they are correct. Then, look for the next weak point and work on that, at the same time trying to retain the success achieved on the previous feature. The better your stock gets, the harder it becomes to retain quality; that's why getting to the top is often easier than staying there!

CONCLUSION

Breeding is what the owner wishes to make of it. It can be little more than random matings of whatever fish are in the tank, right through to an expensive and highly detailed study involving every possible aspect of husbandry. Nothing comes easy to a breeder, least of all good results, so there is bound to be much heartache and frustration along the line. However, the excitement of the unknown makes it an intriguing part of fish-keeping, You are always looking forward to the next spawning to see if your thoughts and efforts will be repaid with some super goldfish. If not, there is always next season and you have enjoyed yourself anyway.

This head-on view of a telescope goldfish accentuates the stalked appearance of the eyes. The more bizarre varieties of goldfish, of which the telescope is actually only moderately strange, often are very difficuft to produce. They may breed poorly and produce only a few fry that closely resemble the parents. Also, it may take months or even years before full development of breed characteristics occurs. Photo: Burkhard Kahl

Goldfish Varieties

It is estimated that there are over 100 varieties of goldfish now bred in various parts of the world, but for all practical purposes there are really only about 15 that you are likely to find in a pet or aquatic store. In many instances, the range may well be restricted to about five or six very popular varieties. The more exotic variants will need to be purchased from specialist breeders, while the rarest varieties may not even be available at all in your country. Many of the rare varieties are restricted to China, Japan, and other eastern countries where the more bizarre forms have a small but loyal band of supporters.

A beautiful broadtail oranda with a high dorsal, square caudal lobes, and nice head growth. This is a breeder of the U.S. strain. Photo: Fred Rosenzweig

The very popular varieties, such as the common goldfish, shubunkins, and comets, will range in price from very inexpensive to moderately priced, depending on their quality. The more exotic could cost you much more, with really outstanding fish exchanging hands for relatively very high prices indeed. This might surprise most people, who think of these fish as being inexpensive. Times have changed and a good goldfish can now, justifiably, command a price related to its quality and the skills that have gone into its breeding.

Those just entering the hobby are strongly advised to gain experience with popular hardy varieties first and progress to the more ornate variants only after they have mastered general aquarium techniques, such as maintaining clear well-oxygenated

A female oranda showing excellent development for its first year of growth. Photo: Tom Caravaglia

Many goldfish breeds are seldom seen. This is the rare edonoshiki, a Japanese calico ranchu. Photo: Fred Rosenzweig

water, feeding, and other aspects of fish husbandry. The more exotic a variety is, the more difficult it will be to maintain; unless one has the time to devote to such fish their initial purchase may be the cause of regret at a later date.

The pond owner should remember that apart from the greater risk of damage to fins and eyes, exotics will not be seen at their best in the more murky waters of a pond. Much of the beauty of such fish will be lost to the viewer.

Before discussing each of the popular varieties, a comment should be made in respect to standards applied to goldfish. A standard is drawn up by a body of interested enthusiasts who form themselves into a society or association. After free discussion, they

Red-capped orandas. Photo: Burkhard Kahl.

will form a show committee whose job is to prepare standards against which goldfish will be judged at shows over which the society in question officiates. With many domesticated pets, over a period of time more than one society will be formed, and as a result there may be two or more official standards. With the passage of time, it often happens that such associations combine to form a single national body that regulates all exhibitions

Below and facing page: Calico pearlscale goldfish with good pearling extending to the back. The fins are long and flowing. The fish below is a show champion. Photo below: Fred Rosenzweig; facing page: Burkhard Kahl

and a single standard is applied. This has occurred in the dog fancy in the USA and the UK, and in the cat fancy in the UK, as well as in the budgerigar and rabbit fancies, for example. However, on other occasions, a single ruling body never becomes a reality; societies go their own way and become deeply entrenched in their own view of what is or is not acceptable within the hobby. There are no less than seven registration bodies (thus standards) applied to cats in the USA, for example.

Very often the difference between the standards is not really so great, but it is within the politics of people within the societies to adopt unbending attitudes, so polarization takes place. This is never in the best interests of the hobby (or rarely so) because it does mean a breeder exhibitor's stock may do well in one society's shows but not in another. It increases an exhibitor's overhead because he or she must join two or more societies, neither of which can offer the level of service that a single unified body could. In order to be fair, the other side of the coin should be stated: this is that single national clubs do sometimes become so large that while they promote the hobby very well, they can sometimes lose touch with the rank and

Top view of a Chinese lionhead. Note the bluntness of the head and the straight back. Photo: Burkhard Kahl

A rare telescope-eyed blue-scale fringetail. Some of the scales up the back almost appear purple. Photo: Fred Rosenzweig

file of the membership. They can be slow to move with the times, and their system for the appointment of judges can come under fire from specialty clubs affiliated with them. Thus break-away societies are formed and some of these succeed while others fall by the wayside. Such may be the evolution within any hobby.

The descriptions used in this chapter are of a general nature. They provide a working guide to the varieties; more detailed information on any given variant should be sought from the ruling body that predominates in your country.

COMMON GOLDFISH

The common goldfish is the original type developed from wild fish by the Chinese. It has remained basically unaltered with the passing centuries, though much refined.

Body

The body is torpedo-shaped and of proportions that most people associate with the typical fish. The

A common goldfish. Just because it is not fancy does not mean it would not make a nice pet. Photo: Fred Rosenzweig

Common goldfish vary greatly in color and even body and fin form but usually are not considered "fancy." Photo: Burkhard Kahl

body depth is ideally 3/7 or 3/8 that of the body length. Viewed from above, the dorsal fin should be straight and in line with the caudal, effectively dividing the body into two exactly equal halves. The maximum width point will be level with the beginning of the dorsal fin and then, still viewed from above, will sweep gently to the end of the peduncle in a smooth curve. Viewed in profile, the maximum depth of the body is from the beginning of the dorsal fin in a line straight down to the underbelly. The peduncle has a depth roughly one third that of the maximum body depth. The head is broad, rounded, and never snipey.

No, this is not a young common goldfish. It is a juvenile long-finned koi, Cyprinus carpio, *Japanese colored carp. Carp and goldfish are closely related but differ in several features, the most obvious being the presence of barbels on the mouth of carp. Photo: Dr. Herbert R. Axelrod*

Fins

There are single dorsal, caudal, and anal fins with paired pectoral and pelvic (or ventral) fins. The dorsal fin should have a maximum height that is about one half that of the body; from this point it should incline in a straight line down to the beginning of the peduncle. The caudal fin is moderately forked and has good-sized lobes, which should be slightly rounded at their ends. The other fins are roughly triangular paddle-shaped and of moderate size.

Colors

The range of available colors is red, orange, yellow, blue, brown, and black. These are termed self colors, meaning that the whole fish is of a single color that should extend into the fins. You can also obtain albino and silver, but these are not liked. Blacks will tend to lose their color as they mature and become a brassy brownish color. The colors are found on metallic scales; they can also be in combination with each other whereby they are termed variegated. It is important that colors are as intense as possible, for any with faded washed-out appearance would make such a goldfish of no value for exhibition or breeding purposes. Color will be at its best in cooler waters; color can fade as a result of bleaching from the sun.

An aquarium containing a selection of the various colors will make a most attractive display. It is also possible to obtain common goldfish which have black edging to their fins. The self colors tend to be the more popular. Those which are variegated should ideally have similar patterns on both sides of the body; this cannot be specifically bred for, so it is a case of looking for those which have such patterns in any given spawning.

This male common goldfish is about five months old. This is the type of fish often purchased in variety stores and put in a goldfish bowl to meet its demise by the age of ten months. No matter what type of goldfish you purchase, at least treat it to an aquarium, not a bowl. Photo: Bob Mertlich

LONDON SHUBUNKIN

The body standard for the London shubunkin is exactly the same as that for the common goldfish, of which it is simply a color variation. In this variety, the scales are of the nacreous type, so they exhibit a pearly sheen to them, or are matt. The base color is blue, and on this are patches of violet, red, orange, yellow, and brown, with numerous spots of black. It is also known as calico (for the printed cloth of that name) and harlequin. The original calicos were produced in Japan. From imports into the UK, they were selectively improved and became known as London, rather than Japanese, shubunkins. The terms calico and harlequin are

A male London shubunkin six months old. Photo: Bob Mertlich

A fairly typical Bristol shubunkin showing the elegant finnage common in this variety.

preferred in the US, though they apply to color patterns rather than scale types. In this variety at least 25% of the body should be blue in color.

BRISTOL SHUBUNKIN

The Bristol shubunkin is named for the city in southwest England where it was originally developed from imports of longfinned fish received from the US; these were crossed with other goldfish and after years of selective breeding, this highly popular fish was given a standard in 1934. In body shape it is the same as the London shubunkin, so it is only seen at shows in nacreous calico form. However, its caudal fin is greatly enlarged and has two very well-rounded lobes to it. Other fins are also larger, so that it is a very elegant fish yet remains a tough variety quite happy in the garden pond. The caudal fin should be held erect with the upper lobe not drooping down. Once again not less than 25% of the color should be blue, and the color should extend

A rather heavily marked and oddly colored Bristol shubunkin. Except for the heavier finnage, this variety is almost identical to the London shubunkin.

into the fins, which will normally be streaked with black with some red-orange included.

When choosing Bristol shubunkins, do not get carried away by young ones exhibiting very large lobes, because once fully mature such fins may be too big and then are likely to droop. Color in any of the shubunkins may take two or more years to become fully established, and during this time it will change steadily. Some young fish can be well marked at an early age but then not be so impressive a few years later. Others get better as they get older. These differences are because color may coalesce with time or it may seem nicely proportioned in a young fish, but as it grows, the proportions are lost and the color appears more sparsely spread over the body.

COMET

The comet is a most elegant goldfish that was developed by Hugo Mulertt in the US during the 1800s. This is the racer of the

Two views of a Bristol shubunkin, Photos: Dr. Herbert R. Axelrod

Color and finnage variations of shubunklns often receive local names and may be quite distinctive. These are Cambridge blue shubunkins. Photo: London Aquatic Society

goldfish, for it has a well-developed caudal fin showing deep forking.

Body

The depth of the body should be about one half, or slightly less, that of the length. Viewed from above it is slightly more flattened than the common goldfish, so it is more streamlined.

Fins

The finnage is the same as the common goldfish but is modified. The dorsal fin is proportionately larger, being about the same height as the body is deep. The angle of the dorsal slope is thus greater than in the common goldfish. The paired fins are of size similar to those in the common variety but may appear larger because the body is more streamlined. The caudal fin lobes should be about 75% as long as the body length—preferably slightly longer but not excessively so, otherwise proportion and propulsion power are lost.

Color

The comet is only exhibited in metallic scale form. It may be red, orange, yellow, blue, brown, or black. Silvers are also available. Yellow is a very well-liked color, and orange in varying shades is also very common. Variegated patterns combining the accepted colors are also available.

There is a variant of the comet which is known as the tancho singletail. This has a circular red disc on its head, the body being silver or white. The word

Another view of a Cambridge blue shubunkin. Photo: London Aquatic Society

tancho is derived from the red disc appearing on the head of the Manchurian crane, and it is one of the basic groupings found in the koi carp. A tancho should have no other color on its body, though invariably red will be found in the fins and traces may be seen on the body of all but outstanding specimens. The tancho should be as circular as possible and not extend beyond the head; otherwise the effect is diminished. You could also call this color pattern a red cap comet or even a hi kabuto, which means red cap or helmet in Japanese. (All terminology in koi is Japanese, and it is quite possible a number of words may find application in goldfish in

Comets are perhaps the most familiar "semifancy" goldfish. The long, pointed lobes on the single (not doubled) tailfin are distinctive. Photo: Bob Mertlich

A five-month-old comet of the type so often seen in pet shops. Photo: Bob Mertlich

the coming years, just as tancho has.)

The comet is a very hardy variety and is quite happy in the garden pond, where the extra space will enable it to display its very fast turn of speed. As with Bristol shubunkins, select youngsters that have nicely proportioned tails so they remain erect when adult. This comment applies to all long-finned goldfish, of which the novice often picks those with enormous finnage; these will not mature into the best fish. The color of the comet, as with other metallics, is not evident until the fish is a few months old, but should be well established by the time it reaches the one year mark or just prior to this. A well-finned and -colored comet is worth a fair price. Poorly colored specimens or over-finned examples are rubbish from an exhibition or breeding viewpoint so

A comet with very long finnage. Photo: Michael Gilroy

should not be costly; they will make useful additions, however, to a pond where the owner is not looking to obtain the very best of examples.

FANTAIL

In the fantail we can see the first movements toward exotic goldfish, for here the body, fins, and eyes may be altered from the normal. Fantails have a long history insomuch as double-tailed fish were known in China centuries ago and were among those exported to Japan around 1500.

Body

In profile, the body is roughly an egg shape with the head end being the more sharply defined and showing a slight indentation at the nape. From above the shape is likewise, but the terminal mouth is blunt. The depth of the body should be slightly greater than 3/5 that of the length.

Fins

In this variety both the anal and caudal fins are double, so the dorsal is the only single fin. The latter rises to be about one half the body depth and it inclines steeply to

A red ryukin. Fantails and ryukins are basically the same variety. Photo: Fred Rosenzweig

the peduncle. The caudal fin is paired and large, though not lobed as in the shubunkin. Viewed from the rear it should appear like a fan, thus the variety's name. The fork in the caudal is only moderate and the lobes should be carried erect, never drooping over, which spoils the effect. The other paired fins are enlarged compared with the common goldfish, but not excessively so.

Eyes

A fantail may have normal or telescope eyes. In the latter, they must be even on both sides of the fish—they appear normal at birth but are developed by about six months of age.

Color

Fantails may be metallic or nacreous scaled. They are available in the full range of colors seen in the

Ryukins or fantails: Above: A calico ryukin. Below: A red and white ryukin. Photos: Dr. Herbert R. Axelrod

A chocolate calico ryukin with very flowing finnage. Photo: Fred Rosenzweig

common goldfish and shubunkins.

The normal-eyed fantails are fine in a pond but are better removed in the colder months in order to protect their finnage. It must be remembered that, apart from atrophy induced by cold weather, long fins are more liable to parasitic attack. Such long-finned fish are also much slower than common goldfish or comets so cannot as easily escape avian or other predators. They make a nice choice for a novice wanting something a little bit more ornate, but this does not imply they are a beginner's fish. Breeding quality fantails is as exacting as with any other variety, and it is necessary to be just as rigid over selection of young to be retained.

VEILTAIL

The veiltail seen in the west today is largely an American- produced variety that was developed from Japanese imports during the 1800s. It is a magnificent goldfish but is not really suited to outdoor ponds, as its superb finnage will soon become ragged and unsightly. This is thus very much an aquarium fish and one which will not grow quite as long as the varieties so far discussed.

Body

As in the fantail, the body is roughly egg-shaped with a depth marginally deeper than the last variety—it should not be less than 2/3 of body length. The caudal peduncle is inclined downwards.

Fins

The fins are as in the fantail but all are much

A rare bronze-colored ryukin. To a specialist, there are subtle distinctions in the caudal fin and body shape that would make this fish resemble a fantail type instead of a typical ryukin. Photo: Fred Rosenzweig

Many ryukins become more colorful as they get older. The fish below is about two years old, while that to the right is about five years old. It is not uncommon for ryukins and other breeds to be almost clean white when very young. Most young goldfish are solid bronzy gold when young, the adult coloration developing slowly over a long period.
Photos: Midori Shobo

A nice young red ryukin with a good deep round body and bright coloration.
Photo: Fred Rosenzweig

A chocolate ryukin. The chocolate-brown coloration is relatively rare in the ryukin breed Photo: Fred Rosenzwelg

A rarity: a black ryukin male showing an excellent deep body.

An excellent calico ryukin with nice form, decent shoulder hump, and very nicely held dosal fin. The blue coloring is nicely developed. Photo: Fred Rosenzweig

A fantastic calico ryukin excellent in form, conformation, and finnage. The shoulder hump is seldom so nice in a calico ryukin. Photo: Fred Rosenzweig

Below: Goldfish often are exhibited by local aquarium clubs and seldom fail to attract attention. Being the owner of a prize-winning goldfish that you have bred yourself is a great boost for the ego. Photo: Dr. Herbert R. Axelrod

A good pair of red and white ryukins with nice coloring on the body and fins.
Photo: Fred Rosenzweig

A red and white ryukin with nice coloration but only fair finnage, including the dorsal fin. The body should have more of a shoulder hump. Photo: Fred Rosenzweig

A true calico veitail showing susceptibility to imperfect water conditions. The bloody fins probably are a reaction to excess ammonia. Photo: Fred Rosenzweig

A rare true white veiltail with nice finnage and good deportment. Unfortunately, the red blood streaks in the tail fin show up most strongly in a white fish. Photo: Fred Rosenzweig

more developed so they are long and flowing. The dorsal should rise high into the water when fully erect and should be as tall as the body is deep. The double caudal fin should trail gracefully and should have a nice clean-cut and straight end to the lobes. The other paired fins are also well developed. The caudal fin in this variety may appear somewhat short in a young fish but should grow to be nicely proportioned. Other fins are slightly more pointed than in the varieties so far covered.

Eyes
The eyes may be normal or telescoped.

Color
Both metallic and nacreous forms are available in self or variegated patterns, as well as calico in the nacreous.

A true calico veitail with a sail-like dorsal fin. Photo: Fred Rosenzweig

The veiltail cannot really be considered a beginner's goldfish, because it is necessary to maintain spotlessly clean water conditions in order to ensure that the delicate fins are not damaged by parasites. Allow plenty of swimming space so the finnage is seen to best effect. Veiltails are not suited to outdoor ponds; even in the aquarium the lower temperatures should not drop below about 12°C (53.5°F). Sometimes in spawnings of fantails and veiltails, single-tails may turn up: these are known as nymphs. They have little value, but some are kept as interesting sports. They should not, however, be used for breeding.

A true calico veitail (without telescope eyes). The high dorsal fin is closely matched by the other fins. The long caudals overlap but are square if held properly. Photo: Fred Rosenzweig

An uncolored veiltail with beautiful caudals and dorsal. The fish has never changed color (as do most goldfish) from its original olive green. Photo: Fred Rosenzweig

GLOBE-EYE TELESCOPE

The globe-eye goldfish is similar to the veiltail but differs in that the caudal fin is forked rather than square cut. The telescopic eyes are truncated cones rather than spherical as in the moor. The globe-eye in its metallic form is only black so could easily be mistaken for a moor; in the nacreous form it is, of course, a mixture of colors with blue as the background. Obtaining black globe-eyed fish is one thing, but maintaining the color is quite another. As in the moor, dense black young fish can start to become brassy brown as they get older. Some may develop silver scales as well, so if you plan to breed with this variety it is important that you purchase from a specialty breeder who has a good strain of blacks. The best outcross for a black is a good deep red fish; this will maintain good intensity of black.

A nice pair of red and white telescope-eye goldfish (also known as globe eyes). The finnage is beautiful and the eyes are uniform. Photo: Fred Rosenzweig

A black and white butterflytail telescope-eye with an attractive color pattern.
Photo: Fred Rosenzweig

A white matt (almost scaleless) telescope-eye broadtail with veitail
characteristics. Photo: Fred Rosenzweig

DEMEKIN

This variety is best described as a telescope-eyed ryukin. It is available in metallic or nacreous forms. The kuro demekin is similar to the moor, for it is a velvet black. Kuro really means a black patch—rather like a tancho—that is seen on the head or, rarely, the dorsal area, but is used in goldfish for the all-black demekin. The metallic red demekins are known as aka demekin, aka meaning red, and is often used to precede other words. If the red were very dark then beni would be more appropriate.

The nacreous form is called sanshoko, which means three colors. Sanke means exactly the same but is an older translation that is used less these days. Nacreous forms of calico invariably carry more than three colors, so

A red and white telescope-eye with a ryukin-type body. Photo: Fred Rosenzweig

Facing page: *A rare mixed breed combination: a black and red telescope-eye oranda fringetail with a beautiful balance of color. Photo: Fred Rosenzweig*

A black and white telescope-eye.
Photo: Fred Rosenzweig

Facing page: Top: a calico butterfly telescope-eye with weak caudal finnage and fair color. Photo: Burkhard Kahl. Bottom: A rare blue-scale and white butterfly telescope-eye. Photo: Fred Rosenzweig

A red and white telescope-eye with a butterfly tail. A 1990 prize-winner. Photo: Fred Rosenzweig

An orange pom-pon telescope-eye with black coloring fading to orange. Pom-pon fully developed. Photo: Fred Rosenzweig

A matt (appears almost scaleless) white butterfly telescope-eye goldfish with a few metallic scales. Photo: Fred Rosenzweig

A rare albino telescope-eye. Note the red iris indicating true albinism, leaving only a washed-out golden coloration; otherwise this is an average fish. Photo: Fred Rosenzweig

*A calico broadtail telescope-eye with good finnage but needing a bulkier body.
Photo: Fred Rosenzweig*

A calico telescope-eye butterfly with an excellent blue-slate gray coloration and little white. The finnage is nice, but the first ray of the dorsal is broken and bloodied. Photo: Fred Rosenzweig

A typical broadtail moor Photo: Burkhard Kahl

the word goshiki, meaning five colors, might be more fitting.

BROADTAIL MOOR

This variety is often incorrectly labeled as the black moor, but this is misleading, as it implies other colored moors are available; if it is not all black, then it is not a moor.

As with the metallic globe-eye, you will see poorly colored examples that carry brown or silvery white. The moor is, of course, a very close relative to the veiltail, of which it is a variety. The telescope eyes appear on the end of spherical appendages, not on truncated cones as in the globe-eye. Sometimes you

Top view of a moor. Note how the telescope eyes bulge outward. Photo: Burkhard Kahl

may see this variety called the veiltail moor, but once again the addition of "veiltail" is unnecessary as a moor is always a veiltailed fish, the caudal fin being square cut, just as in the veiltail.

The moor is obviously not well suited to outdoor situations due to its fins, eyes, and black coloration, the latter of which would make it barely visible against a dark-colored substrate. Good moors are highly prized in goldfish circles. Do not confuse a dark brown veiltail with a moor—look at the eyes to see if they are telescopic. In any case, a dark brown is no substitute for a dense black. When breeding these fish, it is essential to remove any but the blackest of youngsters. The pigment must extend fully into the fins; this makes them a very challenging variety indeed.

A young black moor with imperfect but proudly held dorsal. Photo: Fred Rosenzweig

A rare "peach-colored" pearlscale with excellent scalation. Photo: Fred Rosenzweig

PEARLSCALE

The pearlscale is bodily very similar to the fantail but is distinguished from it in two basic ways. Firstly, its scales are raised like domes—this is the important difference; secondly, the tail fin is smaller and somewhat more rounded in its lobes. The variety was especially developed in England, where it is popular. Although the body has the same shape as the fantail, it will be found that in reality many examples have rather droopy abdomens—almost as though they had dropsy! The domed scales normally have darker outer edges than the center color and this, together with the dome, reflects light in a pearl-like manner.

The color range is wide, being any found in goldfish, and there are both metallic and nacreous types. The latter, of course, always embrace the matt-type scales, which will normally turn

A short-tailed brown pearlscale with nice pearling and excellent golfball-like body. Photo: Fred Rosenzweig

up at the rate of 25% of offspring from matings involving two nacreous parents. The pearlscale is not suited to outdoor ponds, and even in aquariums the lower temperature should not be below about the 14°C (57°F) mark in order to prevent any risk of chilling, for the variety is not as hardy as some others.

As with all other varieties, you will see pearlscales that do not fit the general body standard. This is because there are a considerable number of hybrids sold. Differing fin types appear on bodies not associated with the fins, or pearl scales can appear on fish that do not exhibit the correct body or fins. These are the result of indiscriminate breeding and have no value at all to serious hobbyists, so they should be the least expensive of all goldfish along with those having only poor color.

LIONHEAD

The lionhead is the most exotic goldfish so far discussed, for in this we see one new feature combined with the disappearance of another. In this variety, there is no dorsal fin at all while the head is covered with a raspberry-like growth known as a wen, or hood. In Japan, this fish, known there as the ranchu, is possibly the most highly regarded of all the goldfish and a number of societies are devoted to its cultivation. I do not consider it as elegant or desirable as a good veiltail or comet, but Japanese taste is different. This said, the lionhead also has a very strong following in the West these days. There are clear signs of general internationalism in fish because Japanese tastes are slowly moving towards those of the West, as ours move towards a greater

appreciation of Eastern taste. This is also apparent with koi.

Body

The body is roughly egg-shaped with the depth being greater than half the body length. An elongated body is a bad fault in this variety.

Fins

There is no dorsal fin; other fins are paired—the caudal being divided. The fins of the lionhead are comparatively short and the lobes of the caudal are rounded.

Head

The hood should be as even as possible and should cover the entire head. The hood is divided for allocation of points into the cranial, the infra-orbital, and the opercular regions, the former carrying the most points. It can take up to about three years for the full growth to be complete, but small indications of the lionhead are seen in young fish as tiny wart-like pimples. If the growth is more obvious in the cranial region this is referred to as hooded, whereas if the develop-

Below and Facing Page: Side and top views of a Chinese lionhead. Photos: Fred Rosenzweig.

Above: A Chinese pom-pon lionhead.
Right: An interesting pair of ranchus.
Photos: Fred Rosenzweig

ment is greater in the orbital region it is known as okame. The lionhead is more restricted in its movements due to the head growth.

Color

Lionheads are available in both metallic and nacreous forms so the full color range is possible. The nacreous forms are called edonishiki (nishiki being printed colored cloths or woven silks imported to Japan from India; omit the second "i" for pronunciation).

The lionhead can be put into garden ponds but only during the warmer months. Do take extra care to see that such fish are individually fed, because if they are in company they just will be unable to compete with normally finned fish. This is not a beginner's fish, because the hood requires careful observation to keep it free of parasitic or fungal attack. Also, due to the restricted gill movements, the water must be well oxygenated. All varieties that have no dorsal fin will be poor swimmers, as they have difficulty in balancing correctly. The fact that their bodies are short and rather spherical does not help matters.

Lionheads imported from Japan will tend to have a more downwardly inclined peduncle than many produced in the West, for the Japanese prefer the caudal fin to be lower down. In fact, in Japan there are

various strains which show slight deviations from each other.

RANCHU

The ranchu is the lionhead of Japan, so it is similar in all respects to the description of this latter variety. Differences are that the dorsal curve is more domed and sweeps to a more downwardly pointing pecluncle. The Osaka ranchu is very different inasmuch as there is no raspberry-like head growth or hood, the head being normal and somewhat pointed; the Nankin ranchu is similar to the Osaka and has a silver body with red tips and fins. These variations lacking the hood, or wen, are not as popular today in Japan as in past years.

Below and Facing page: White and red ranchus. Photo: Fred Rosenzweig

ORANDA

The oranda is best described as a veiltail with a lion head, for it combines both features. The veiltail is of the globe-eye type in that it is forked and not squarecut at its extremity. The eyes are of the normal type. The hood is not usually as well developed as in the lionhead variety. It is a handsome fish, but having both a hood and long fins does mean it is better kept in the aquarium (with the lower temperature restricted to that given for the other delicate varieties). This variety is seen in both metallic and nacreous forms, the latter being known as azumanishiki. An additional important variety is the redcap oranda. This term is gradually being replaced with the Japanese term: tancho. I think it is more appropriate to use Japanese terms, for it will be found that many of them are more specific than if translations are done, which do not always have quite the intended meaning in the West.

The tancho is a silver or white fish with the red restricted to the head, where it ideally should form as near to a circle as possible.

An excellent calico oranda that is very well balanced and has excellent overall finnage. The body shape is muscular and round, and the head and head growth are excellent. Although lacking blue, the coloration is very good and distinct. Photo: Fred Rosenzweig

A very high quality redcap oranda with a totally white body and full long fins. The red head growth is confined to above the eyeline. A superb fish. Photo: Fred Rosenzweig

No other color should appear in the goldfish. You will often find, however, that at the edges of the tancho it is yellow or orange. If the red extends into the nape then it can no longer be correctly termed a tancho. Because the pattern in this variety is so basic, it is equally important that the body color be as even and white, or silver, as possible. Another word having the same meaning as tancho is hinomaru, which is the red circle representing the rising sun on Japan's national flag.

In the case of all colors except for the tancho, they should extend into the fins.

Although the novice may be tempted to purchase the glamorous oranda, the urge is better avoided until good experience has been gained with the more hardy varieties; to do otherwise is really not fair to these more delicate fish.

POM-PON

The feature of the pompon is the excessive development of the nasal septa, the nostrils of the goldfish. Such growths are called narial bouquets. The extent of the growths varies considerably from mildly to very much so; in some cases the pom-pons dangle in front of the mouth and are sucked in and out.

Closeup of a pom-pon celestial. Celestials have the eyes looking upward. Pom-pons are rare in celestials. Photo: Fred Rosenzweig

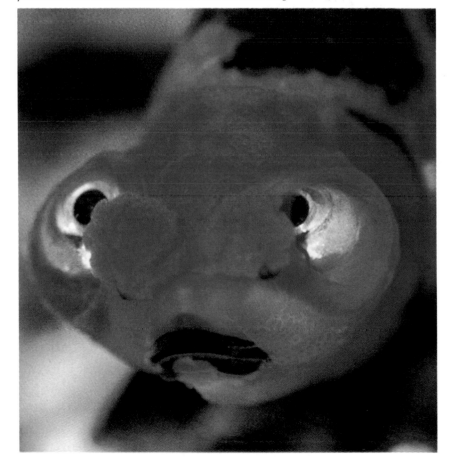

A pom-pon oranda. Notice the bending of the gill cover, a frequent genetic flaw. Photo: Fred Rosenzweig

I have to say I find these grotesque examples beyond reasonable limits, but the variety clearly appeals to a number of people. While not that popular, these fish do have a dedicated band of devotees.

The pom-pon may have full finnage or no dorsal fin; the body is of the short egg-shape type. The septa should be developed evenly. All colors and scale types are available. They are hardy fish so can cope well enough in ponds, but this is not advised, as the delicate nasal membranes could easily be subject to parasitic attack if not observed on a regular basis and not kept in water of the highest quality—which is much more difficult in pond situations.

CELESTIAL

In the celestial, as the name suggests, the eyes look skyward, giving the fish a very strange appearance indeed. The variety is of Chinese origin. Even into this century, it was advocated that to keep these fish one needed to black out the aquarium sides so the fish was encouraged to look upwards. This, of course, is rubbish because the abnormality is purely genetic; any improvement (if this is a suitable choice of word!) can only be made by breeding. The celestial has no dorsal fin and only poorly developed finnage—which is paired, the caudal fin being divided.

Top view of a fixed-eyed celestial. Photo: Michael Gilroy

Top view of a celestial with the typical upturned eyes. Photo: Klaus Paysan.

suited to the outdoor pond. Indeed, even in an aquarium its eyes are very prone to damage, so it must always be cared for with this in mind. It will have difficulty seeing food once the food falls below it; it is amazing that the celestial can eat as well as it does. This is not a variety I would ever recommend, simply on practical grounds—without any consideration to ethical aspects, on which we all have differing views.

The body is short and the depth should be greater than half the length. Both metallic and nacreous forms are available in the full range of colors seen in goldfish. When the fish are young, the eyes are normal, rather like telescopic eyes, but as the fish mature the eyes turn upwards. It is important that they should develop evenly on both sides of the head and that they are well matched. Ideally they must be at a 90° angle to the body.

This is obviously a very delicate variety so is not

BUBBLE-EYE

In this variety we move from the bizarre to the grotesque in many people's view (including my own). The bubble-eye's main feature is obviously the fact that under each eye there develops a sac which fills with fluid; these sway as the fish swims. In actual fact, although superficially similar to the celestial,

there is a small difference in respect to the eyes. Although they look upwards, it will be found that they are inclined eyes rather than true upward-facing eyes. There is no dorsal fin and the other finnage is paired, with the caudal divided. The fins are also better developed in most examples.

Again, this is not a fish for either the pond or the novice. The eye sacs are easily damaged, so it is important that no sharp objects—such as rocks—are in the tank, though the eye sacs do repair themselves if accidents occur. I am told that in spite of their obvious deficiencies, this variety copes quite well in a mixed community, as its other senses compensate for any lack of vision. (This being equally as true of the celestial.) The body of this variety is similar to that of this latter fish, and the same range of colors is available in the differing reflective types.

OTHER VARIETIES

The varieties discussed are those that will be seen in aquatic shops and stocked by the more specialized dealer, but as previously mentioned, the full list of goldfish would run to over 100 and is being added to each year. Some were popular in China and Japan years ago but then lost followers; they are now enjoying somewhat of a comeback as more breeders in the West search for something different. Dealers, too, always have an eye for a variety that might give their particular list extra individuality, so you may see all sorts of unheard of names being tagged onto goldfish. There is the meteor, which is an egg-shaped fish with no caudal fin but very well developed pelvic and anal fins. There is the tiger head, which is a veiltail or fringetail sporting pom-pons, and

A tosakin.

there is the dragon fish, with telescope eyes and pom-pons. The curl-gilled goldfish has gills (or rather gill covers) that turn outward and this mutation can be combined with others. In fact, if one mutation is introduced to another variety, it creates a new variety and a new name; likewise, additional scale types to a variety will thus form another type which is regarded as a separate variety. As with many other pets, it can become complex keeping track of what names mean because they are often used indiscriminately by some breeders wishing to promote their fish as having some special feature.

Although different groups of pet owners often believe

what is happening in their sphere of interest is perhaps unique, this is not actually so. For example, it is presently very "fashionable" in nearly all pet groups to be adding new "breeds" or varieties. Many of these will never become really popular simply because, in truth, they are no more than genetic degenerates that have numerous problems. It is actually far easier to propagate a line of new mutants than it is to improve an already excellent variety. Herein, maybe, can be found the reason why so many new varieties are appearing. Many young breeders want success instantly, rather than learning the art of animal rearing and breeding by carefully upgrading sound stock. It is much easier to show a fish few people have ever heard of than to display stock of a variety that many long-time experts can easily judge.

Caution should be exercised with new varieties because the further they deviate from the essential basics of a goldfish, the harder they will be to breed and care for. One could finish up with a much pampered piece of living organism that is so delicate that it must be retained in ultra-hygienic aquariums in which there are no rocks or gravel or plants. That is not what aquaculture is all about, so people soon tire of the novelty and leave the hobby.

On the other hand, selectively trying to improve a sound, vigorous variety that can be maintained in a fully set-up aquarium is a real challenge which provides great beauty as well. Within the popular varieties that have stood the test of time, there is still much to do. Color breeding in goldfish is still in its infancy and offers the newcomer—tomorrows's expert—a whole dimension to try and develop beautiful patterns and color combinations on the goldfish.

Index